D0720238

THE OFFICIAL
Raspberry Pi
Beginner's Guide
How to use your new computer

First published in 2019 by Raspberry Pi Trading Ltd, Maurice Wilkes Building,
St. John's Innovation Park, Cowley Road, Cambridge, CB4 0DS

Publishing Director: Russell Barnes • Editor: Phil King • Sub Editor: Nicola King
Design: Critical Media • Illustrations: Sam Alder
CEO: Eben Upton

ISBN: 978-1-912047-58-1

Welcome to the Official Raspberry Pi Beginner's Guide

We think you're going to love Raspberry Pi. This ultra-small, affordable computer costs less than most video games, but can be used to learn coding, build robots, and create all kinds of weird and wonderful projects.

Raspberry Pi is capable of doing all the things you'd expect from a computer – everything from browsing the internet and playing games, to watching movies and listening to music. But Raspberry Pi is much more than a modern computer.

With a Raspberry Pi you can get into the heart of a computer. You get to set up your own operating system, and can connect wires and circuits directly to the pins on its board. It was designed to teach young people how to program in languages like Scratch and Python, and all the major programming languages are included with the official operating system.

The world needs programmers more than ever, and Raspberry Pi has ignited a love of computer science and technology in a new generation.

People of all ages use Raspberry Pi to create exciting projects: everything from retro games consoles to internet-connected weather stations.

So if you want to make games, build robots, or hack a variety of amazing projects, then this book is here to help you get started.

About the Author

Gareth Halfacree is a freelance technology journalist, writer, and former system administrator in the education sector. With a passion for open-source software and hardware, he was an early adopter of the Raspberry Pi platform and has written several publications on its capabilities and flexibility. He can be found on Twitter as **@ghalfacree** or via his website at **freelance.halfacree.co.uk**.

Contents

Chapter 1

Get to know your Raspberry Pi

Get fully acquainted with your new credit-card-sized computer by taking a guided tour of Raspberry Pi. Discover its numerous components and what they do

Raspberry Pi is a remarkable device: a fully functional computer in a tiny and low-cost package. Whether you're looking for a device you can use to browse the web or play games, are interested in learning how to write your own programs, or are looking to create your own circuits and physical devices, Raspberry Pi – and its amazing community – will support you every step of the way.

Raspberry Pi is known as a *single-board computer*, which means exactly what it sounds like: it's a computer, just like a desktop, laptop, or smartphone, but built on a single *printed circuit board*. Like most single-board computers, Raspberry Pi is small – roughly the same footprint as a credit card – but that doesn't mean it's not powerful: a Raspberry Pi can do anything a bigger and more power-hungry computer can do, though not necessarily as quickly.

The Raspberry Pi family was born from a desire to encourage more hands-on computer education around the world. Its creators, who joined together to form the non-profit Raspberry Pi Foundation, had little idea that it would prove so popular: the few thousand built in 2012 to test the waters were immediately sold out, and millions have been shipped all over the world in the years since. These boards have found their ways into homes, classrooms, offices, data centres, factories, and even self-piloting boats and spacefaring balloons.

Various models of Raspberry Pi have been released since the original Model B, each bringing either improved specifications or features specific to a particular use-case. The Raspberry Pi Zero family, for example, is a tiny version of the full-size Raspberry Pi which drops a few features – in particular the multiple USB ports and wired network port – in favour of a significantly smaller layout and reduced power requirements.

All Raspberry Pi models have one thing in common, though: they're *compatible*, meaning that software written for one model will run on any other model. It's even possible to take the very latest version of Raspberry Pi's operating system and run it on an original pre-launch Model B prototype. It will run more slowly, it's true, but it will still run.

Throughout this book you'll be learning about Raspberry Pi 4 Model B, the latest and most powerful version of Raspberry Pi. What you learn, though, can be easily applied to other models in the Raspberry Pi family, so don't worry if you're using a different version.

A guided tour of Raspberry Pi

Unlike a traditional computer, which hides its inner workings in a case, Raspberry Pi has all its components, ports, and features out on display – although you can buy a case to provide extra protection, if you'd prefer. This makes it a great tool for learning about what the various parts of a computer do, and also makes it easy to learn what goes where when it comes time to plug in the various extras – known as *peripherals* – you'll need to get started.

Figure 1-1 (overleaf) shows a Raspberry Pi 4 Model B as seen from above. When you're using a Raspberry Pi with this book, try to keep it turned the same way as in the picture; if it's turned around it can get confusing when it comes to using things like the GPIO header (detailed in **Chapter 6, Physical computing with Scratch and Python**).

◄ **Figure 1-1:** Raspberry Pi 4 Model B

While it may look like there's a lot packed into the tiny board, a Raspberry Pi is very simple to understand — starting with its *components*, the inner workings that make the device tick.

Raspberry Pi's components

Like any computer, Raspberry Pi is made up of various components, each of which has a role to play in making it work. The first, and arguably most important, of these can be found just above the centre point on the top side of the board (**Figure 1-2**), covered in a metal cap: the *system-on-chip* (SoC).

▲ **Figure 1-2:** Raspberry Pi's system-on-chip (SoC)

The name system-on-chip is a great indicator of what you would find if you prised the metal cover off: a silicon chip, known as an *integrated circuit,* which contains the bulk of Raspberry Pi's system. This includes the *central processing unit* (CPU), commonly thought of as the 'brain' of a computer, and the *graphics processing unit* (GPU), which handles the visual side of things.

A brain is no good without memory, however, and just to side of the SoC you'll find exactly that: another chip, which looks like a small, black, plastic square (**Figure 1-3**). This is Raspberry Pi's *random access memory (RAM)*. When you're working on Raspberry Pi, it's the RAM that holds what you're doing; only when you save your work will it be written to the microSD card. Together, these components form Raspberry Pi's volatile and non-volatile memories: the volatile RAM loses its contents whenever Raspberry Pi is powered off, while the non-volatile microSD card keeps its contents.

▲ **Figure 1-3:** Raspberry Pi's random access memory (RAM)

A the top right of the board you'll find another metal lid (**Figure 1-4**, overleaf) covering the *radio*, the component which gives Raspberry Pi the ability to communicate with devices wirelessly. The radio itself acts as two main components, in fact: a *WiFi radio*, for connecting to computer networks; and a *Bluetooth radio*, for connecting to peripherals like mice and for sending data to or receiving data from nearby smart devices like sensors or smartphones.

▲ **Figure 1-4:** Raspberry Pi's radio module

Another black, plastic-covered chip can be seen to the bottom edge of the board, just behind the middle set of USB ports. This is the *USB controller*, and is responsible for running the four USB ports. Next to this is an even smaller chip, the *network controller*, which handles Raspberry Pi's Ethernet network port. A final black chip, smaller than the rest, can be found a little bit above the USB Type-C power connector to the upper-left of the board (**Figure 1-5**); this is known as a *power management integrated circuit (PMIC)*, and handles turning the power that comes in from the micro USB port into the power Raspberry Pi needs to run.

▲ **Figure 1-5:** Raspberry Pi's power management integrated circuit (PMIC)

Don't worry if this seems like a lot to take in; you don't need to know what each component is or where to find it on the board in order to use Raspberry Pi.

Raspberry Pi's ports

Raspberry Pi has a range of ports, starting with four *Universal Serial Bus (USB) ports*
(**Figure 1-6**) to the middle and right-hand side of the bottom edge. These ports let you connect
any USB-compatible peripheral, from keyboards and mice to digital cameras and flash drives,
to Raspberry Pi. Speaking technically, there are two types of USB ports: the ones with black
parts inside are USB 2.0 ports, based on version two of the Universal Serial Bus standard; the
ones with blue parts are faster USB 3.0 ports, based on the newer version three.

▲ **Figure 1-6:** Raspberry Pi's USB ports

To the right of the USB ports is an *Ethernet port*, also known as a *network port* (**Figure 1-7**).
You can use this port to connect Raspberry Pi to a wired computer network using a cable with
what is known as an RJ45 connector on its end. If you look closely at the Ethernet port, you'll
see two light-emitting diodes (LEDs) at the bottom; these are status LEDs, and let you know
that the connection is working.

▲ **Figure 1-7:** Raspberry Pi's Ethernet port

Just above the Ethernet port, on the left-hand edge of Raspberry Pi, is a *3.5 mm audio-visual (AV) jack* (**Figure 1-8**). This is also known as the *headphone jack*, and it can be used for that exact purpose – though you'll get better sound connecting it to amplified speakers rather than headphones. It has a hidden, extra feature, though: as well as audio, the 3.5 mm AV jack carries a video signal which can be connected to TVs, projectors, and other displays that support a *composite video signal* using a special cable known as a *tip-ring-ring-sleeve (TRRS)* adapter.

▲ **Figure 1-8:** Raspberry Pi's 3.5 mm AV jack

Directly above the 3.5 mm AV jack is a strange-looking connector with a plastic flap which can be pulled up; this is the *camera connector*, also known as the *Camera Serial Interface (CSI)* (**Figure 1-9**). This allows you to use the specially designed Raspberry Pi Camera Module (about which you'll learn more in **Chapter 8, Raspberry Pi Camera Module**.)

▲ **Figure 1-9:** Raspberry Pi's camera connector

Above that, still on the left-hand edge of the board, are the *micro High Definition Multimedia Interface (micro-HDMI) ports*, which are a smaller version of the connectors you'll find on a games console, set-top box, or TV (**Figure 1-10**). The multimedia part of its name tells you that it carries both audio and video signals, while high-definition tells you that you can expect excellent quality. You'll use these to connect Raspberry Pi to one or two display devices: a computer monitor, TV, or projector.

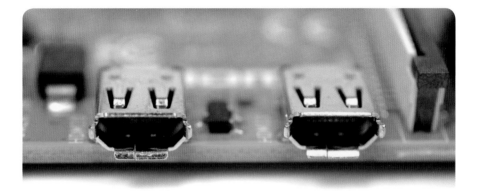

▲ **Figure 1-10:** Raspberry Pi's micro-HDMI ports

Above the HDMI ports is a *USB Type-C power port* (**Figure 1-11**), which you'll use to connect Raspberry Pi to a power source. The USB Type-C port is a common sight on smartphones, tablets, and other portable devices. While you could use a standard mobile charger to power Raspberry Pi, for best results you should use the official Raspberry Pi USB Type-C Power Supply.

▲ **Figure 1-11:** Raspberry Pi's USB Type-C power port

At the top edge of the board is another strange-looking connector (**Figure 1-12**), which at first glance appears to be identical to the camera connector. This, though, is the exact opposite: a *display connector*, or *Display Serial Interface (DSI)*, designed for use with a Raspberry Pi Touch Display (**Figure 1-13**).

▲ **Figure 1-12:** Raspberry Pi's display connector (DSI)

▲ **Figure 1-13:** The Raspberry Pi Touch Display

At the right-hand edge of the board you'll find 40 metal pins, split into two rows of 20 pins (**Figure 1-14**). This is the *GPIO (general-purpose input/output) header*, a feature of Raspberry Pi used to talk to additional hardware from LEDs and buttons all the way to temperature sensors, joysticks, and pulse-rate monitors. You'll learn more about the GPIO header in **Chapter 6, Physical computing with Scratch and Python**. Just below and to the left of this header is another, smaller header with four pins: this is used to connect the Power over Ethernet (PoE) HAT, an optional add-on which lets Raspberry Pi receive power from a network connection rather than the USB Type-C port.

▲ **Figure 1-14:** Raspberry Pi's GPIO header

There's one final port on Raspberry Pi, but you won't see it on the top. Turn the board over and you'll find a *microSD card connector* on the opposite side of the board to the display connector (**Figure 1-15**). This is Raspberry Pi's storage: the microSD card inserted in here contains all the files you save, all the software you install, and the operating system that makes Raspberry Pi run.

▲ **Figure 1-15:** Raspberry Pi's microSD card connector

Raspberry Pi's peripherals

A Raspberry Pi by itself can't do very much, just the same as a desktop computer on its own is little more than a door-stop. To work, Raspberry Pi needs peripherals: at the minimum, you'll need a microSD card for storage; a monitor or TV so you can see what you're doing; a keyboard and mouse to tell Raspberry Pi what to do; and a 5 volt (5 V) USB Type-C power supply rated at 3 amps (3 A) or better. With those, you've got yourself a fully functional computer. You'll learn how to connect all these peripherals to your Raspberry Pi in **Chapter 2, Getting started with your Raspberry Pi**.

Those aren't the end of the peripherals you can use with your Raspberry Pi, though. Official accessories produced by the Raspberry Pi Foundation include: the Raspberry Pi Case, which helps protect the Pi while you're using it without blocking your access to its various ports; the Camera Module, detailed in **Chapter 8, Raspberry Pi Camera Module**; the Raspberry Pi Touch Display, which connects to the display port and provides both a video display and a tablet-style touchscreen interface; and the Sense HAT (**Figure 1-16**), a clever multifunctional add-on which is detailed in full in **Chapter 7, Physical computing with the Sense HAT**.

A wide assortment of third-party accessories are also available, ranging from kits to turn Raspberry Pi into a laptop or tablet to add-ons which give it the ability to understand your speech and even talk back to you. While it's tempting to run out and fill a shopping trolley, though, remember that you'll need to learn to walk with your Raspberry Pi before taking on the hardware equivalent of a marathon!

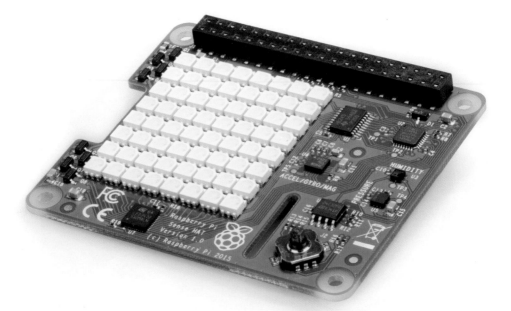

▲ **Figure 1-16:** The Sense HAT

Chapter 2

Getting started with your Raspberry Pi

Discover the essential items you'll need for your Raspberry Pi and how to connect them all to get it set up and working

Raspberry Pi has been designed to be as quick and easy to set up and use as possible, but – like any computer – it relies on various external components, called *peripherals*. While it's easy to take a look at the bare circuit board of Raspberry Pi – which looks significantly different to the encased, closed-off computers you may be used to – and worry things are about to get complicated, that's not the case. You can be up and running with Raspberry Pi in well under ten minutes simply by following the steps in this guide.

If you have received this book as part of a Raspberry Pi Starter Kit, then you'll already have almost everything you'll need to get started: all you need to provide is a computer monitor or TV with an HDMI connection – the same type of connector used by set-top boxes, Blu-ray players, and games consoles – so you can see what your Raspberry Pi is doing.

If you don't have a Raspberry Pi Starter Kit, then in addition to a Raspberry Pi 4 Model B you'll need:

■ **USB power supply** – A 5 V power supply rated at 3 amps (3 A) and with a USB Type-C connector. The Official Raspberry Pi Power Supply is the recommended choice, as it can cope with the quickly switching power demands of Raspberry Pi.

■ **microSD card with NOOBS** – The microSD card acts as Raspberry Pi's permanent storage; all the files you create and software you install, along with the operating system itself, are stored on the card. An 8GB card will get you started, though a 16GB one offers more room to grow. Using a card with NOOBS, the New Out-Of-Box Software, pre-installed will save you time; otherwise see **Appendix A** for instructions on installing NOOBS on a blank card.

■ **USB keyboard and mouse** – The keyboard and mouse allow you to control your Raspberry Pi. Almost any wired or wireless keyboard and mouse with a USB connector will work with Raspberry Pi, though some 'gaming' style keyboards with colourful lights may draw too much power to be used reliably.

■ **Micro-HDMI cable** – This carries sound and images from Raspberry Pi to your TV or monitor. One end of the cable has a micro-HDMI connector for Raspberry Pi; the other, a full-size HDMI connector for your display. Or, you can use a micro-HDMI to HDMI adapter and a standard, full-size HDMI cable. If using a monitor without an HDMI socket, you can buy micro-HDMI to DVI-D, DisplayPort, or VGA adapters. To connect to an older TV which uses composite video or has a SCART socket, use a 3.5 mm tip-ring-ring-sleeve (TRRS) audio/video cable.

Raspberry Pi is safe to use without a case, providing you don't place it on a metal surface which could conduct electricity and cause a short-circuit. An optional case, however, can provide additional protection; the Starter Kit includes the Official Raspberry Pi Case, while third-party cases are available from all good stockists.

If you want to use Raspberry Pi on a wired network, rather than a wireless (WiFi) network, you'll also need a network cable. This should be connected at one end to your network's switch or router. If you're planning to use Raspberry Pi's built-in wireless radio, you won't need a cable; you will, however, need to know the name and key or passphrase for your wireless network.

Setting up the hardware

Begin by unpacking your Raspberry Pi from its box. Raspberry Pi is a robust piece of hardware, but that doesn't mean it's indestructible: try to get into the habit of holding the board by the edges, rather than on its flat sides, and be extra careful around the raised metal pins. If these pins are bent, at best it'll make using add-on boards and other extra hardware difficult and, at worst, can cause a short-circuit that will damage your Raspberry Pi.

If you haven't done so already, have a look at **Chapter 1, Getting to know your Raspberry Pi**, for details on exactly where the various ports are and what they do.

Assembling the case

If you're installing Raspberry Pi in a case, it should be your first step. If you're using the Official Raspberry Pi Case, begin by splitting it into its two individual pieces: the red base and white lid.

1 Take the base and hold it so that the raised end is to your left and the lower end to your right.

2 Holding your Raspberry Pi (with no microSD card inserted) by its USB and Ethernet ports, at a slight angle, slot its connectors (USB Type-C, 2 × micro-HDMI, and 3.5 mm) into their holes in the side of the base, then gently lower the other side down so it sits flat.

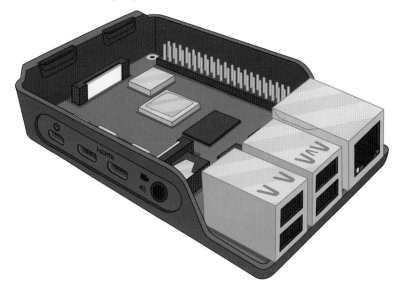

3 Take the white lid and place the two clips at the left into the matching holes on the left of the base, above the microSD card slot. When they're in place, push the right-hand side (above the USB ports) down until you hear a click.

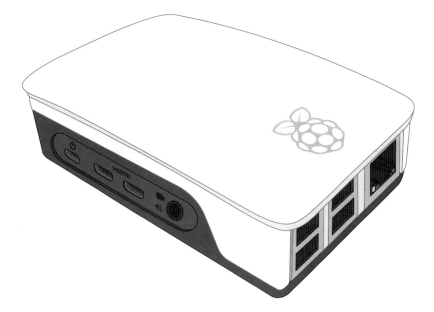

Connecting the microSD card

To install the microSD card, which is Raspberry Pi's *storage*, turn Raspberry Pi (in its case if using one) over and slide the card into the microSD slot with the label facing away from Raspberry Pi. It can only go in one way, and should slide home without too much pressure.

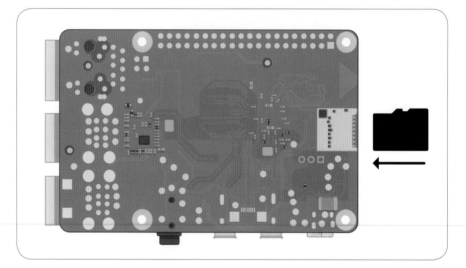

The microSD card will slide into the connector, then stop without a click.

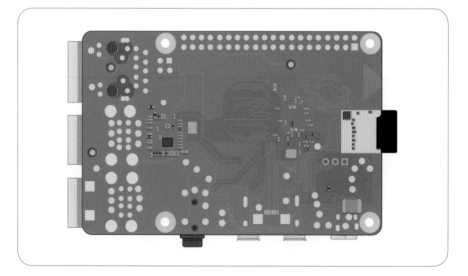

If you want to remove it again in the future, simply grip the end of the card and pull it gently out. If you're using an older model of Raspberry Pi, you'll need to give the card a gentle push first to unlock it; this isn't necessary with a Raspberry Pi 3 or 4.

Connecting a keyboard and mouse

Connect the keyboard's USB cable to any of the four USB ports (2.0 or 3.0) on Raspberry Pi. If you're using the Official Raspberry Pi Keyboard, there's a USB port on the back for the mouse; if not, just connect your mouse's USB cable from your mouse to another USB port on Raspberry Pi.

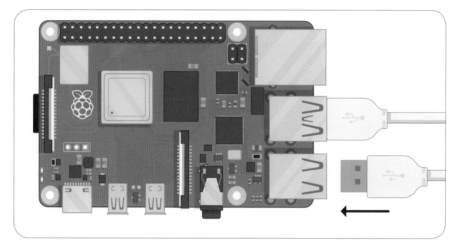

The USB connectors for the keyboard and mouse should slide home without too much pressure; if you're having to force the connector in, there's something wrong. Check that the USB connector is the right way up!

KEYBOARD & MOUSE

The keyboard and mouse act as your main means of telling Raspberry Pi what to do; in computing, these are known as *input devices*, in contrast with the display which is an *output device*.

Connecting a display

Take the micro-HDMI cable and connect the smaller end to the micro-HDMI port closest to the USB Type-C port on your Raspberry Pi, and the other end to your display. If your display has more than one HDMI port, look for a port number next to the connector itself; you'll need to switch the TV to this input to see Raspberry Pi's display. If you can't see a port number, don't worry: you can simply switch through each input in turn until you find Raspberry Pi.

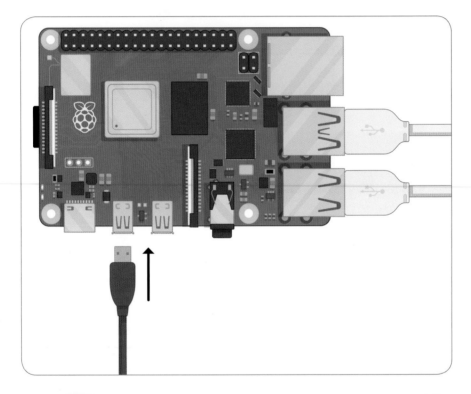

TV CONNECTION

If your TV or monitor doesn't have an HDMI connector, that doesn't mean you can't use Raspberry Pi. Adapter cables, available from any electronics stockist, will allow you to convert the micro-HDMI port on Raspberry Pi to DVI-D, DisplayPort, or VGA for use with older computer monitors; these are simply connected to Raspberry Pi's micro-HDMI port, then a suitable cable used to connect the adapter cable to the monitor. If your TV has only a composite video or SCART input, you can purchase 3.5 mm tip-ring-ring-sleeve (TRRS) adapter cables and composite-to-SCART adapters which connect to the 3.5 mm AV jack.

Connecting a network cable (optional)

To connect your Raspberry Pi to a wired network, take a network cable – known as an Ethernet cable – and push it into Raspberry Pi's Ethernet port, with the plastic clip facing downwards, until you hear a click. If you need to remove the cable, just squeeze the plastic clip inwards towards the plug and gently slide the cable free again.

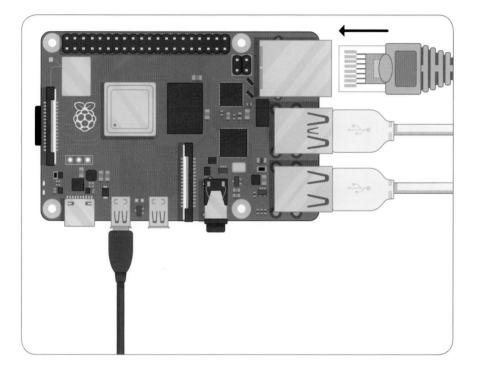

The other end of your network cable should be connected to any free port on your network hub, switch, or router in the same way.

Connecting a power supply

Connecting Raspberry Pi to a power supply is the very last step in the hardware setup process, and it's one you should do only when you're ready to set up its software: Raspberry Pi does not have a power switch and will turn on as soon as it is connected to a live power supply.

First, connect the USB Type-C end of the power supply cable to the USB Type-C power connector on Raspberry Pi. It can go in either way around and should slide home gently. If your power supply has a detachable cable, make sure the other end is plugged into the body of the power supply.

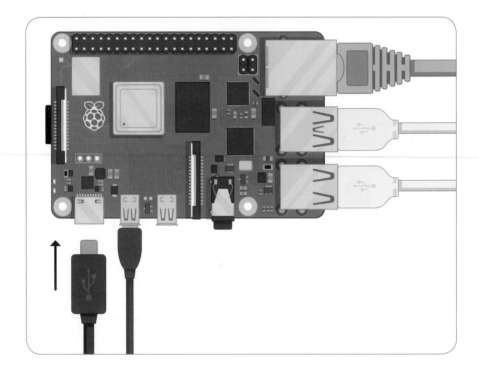

Finally, connect the power supply to a mains socket and switch the socket on; your Raspberry Pi will immediately start running.

Congratulations: you have put your Raspberry Pi together!

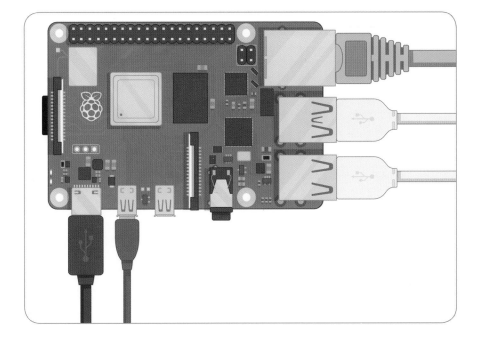

You'll briefly see four Raspberry Pi logos at the top left of a black screen, and may see a blue screen appear as the software resizes itself to make full use of your microSD card. If you see a black screen, wait a few minutes; the first time Raspberry Pi boots it has to do some housekeeping in the background. After a while you'll see the Raspbian desktop and setup wizard, as in **Figure 2-1**. Your operating system is now ready to be configured, which you'll learn to do in **Chapter 3, Using your Raspberry Pi**.

▲ **Figure 2-1:** The Raspbian desktop and setup wizard

Chapter 3
Using your Raspberry Pi

Learn about the Raspbian operating system

R aspberry Pi is able to run a wide range of software, including a number of different operating systems – the core software that makes a computer run. The most popular of these, and the official operating system of the Raspberry Pi Foundation, is Raspbian. Based on Debian Linux, Raspbian is tailor-made for Raspberry Pi and comes with a range of extras pre-installed and ready to go.

If you've only ever used Microsoft Windows or Apple macOS, don't worry: Raspbian is based on the same windows, icons, menus, and pointer (WIMP) principles, and should quickly feel familiar. The following chapter will get you started and introduce you to some of the bundled software.

The Welcome Wizard

The first time you run Raspbian, you'll see the Welcome Wizard (**Figure 3-1**). This helpful tool will walk you through changing some settings in Raspbian, known as the *configuration*, to match how and where you will be using Raspberry Pi.

▲ **Figure 3-1:** The Welcome Wizard

CLOSING THE WIZARD

You can choose to close the Welcome Wizard by clicking the Cancel button, but certain Raspberry Pi features – such as the wireless network – won't work until you answer at least the first set of questions.

Click the Next button, then choose your country, language, and time zone by clicking on each drop-down box in turn and selecting your answer from the list (**Figure 3-2**). If you are using a US-layout keyboard, click on the check box to make sure Raspbian uses the correct keyboard layout. If you want the desktop and programs to appear in English, regardless of your country's native language, click on the 'Use English language' checkbox to tick it. When you're finished, click Next.

▲ **Figure 3-2:** Selecting a language, among other options

The next screen will ask you to change the password for the 'pi' user (from the default 'raspberry') – for security purposes, it's a very good idea to create a new one. Enter it in the boxes (**Figure 3-3**). You can click on the tick next to 'Hide characters' to show the passwords, which must be the same in both boxes. When you're happy, click Next.

▲ **Figure 3-3:** Setting a new password

The next screen will allow you to choose your WiFi network from a list (**Figure 3-4**). Scroll through the list of networks with the mouse or keyboard, find your network's name, click on it, then click Next. Assuming that your wireless network is secure (it really should be), you'll be asked for its password, also known as its pre-shared key; this is normally written on a card with the router or on the bottom of the router itself. Click Next to connect to the network. If you don't want to connect to a wireless network, just click Skip.

▲ **Figure 3-4:** Choosing a wireless network

WIRELESS NETWORKING

Built-in wireless networking is only available on the Raspberry Pi 3, Pi 4, and Pi Zero W families. If you want to use another model of Raspberry Pi with a wireless network, you'll need a USB WiFi adapter.

The next screen will allow you to check for and install updates for Raspbian and the other software on Raspberry Pi (**Figure 3-5**). Raspbian is regularly updated to fix bugs, add new features, and improve performance. To install these updates, click Next; otherwise, click Skip. Downloading the updates can take several minutes, so be patient. When the updates are installed, a window saying 'System is up to date' will appear; click the OK button.

▲ **Figure 3-5:** Checking for updates

The final screen of the Welcome Wizard (**Figure 3-6**) has a simple task to do: certain changes made will only take effect when you restart your Raspberry Pi, a process known as rebooting. If prompted to do so, click the Reboot button and Raspberry Pi will restart. This time the Welcome Wizard won't appear; its job is done, and your Raspberry Pi is ready to use.

▲ **Figure 3-6:** Rebooting Raspberry Pi

Navigating the desktop

The version of Raspbian installed on most Raspberry Pi boards is properly known as 'Raspbian with desktop,' referring to its main graphical user interface (**Figure 3-7**). The bulk of this desktop is taken up with a picture, known as the wallpaper (**A** in **Figure 3-7**), on top of which the programs you run will appear. At the top of the desktop is a taskbar (**B**), which allows you to actually load each of the programs; these are then indicated by tasks (**C**) in the taskbar.

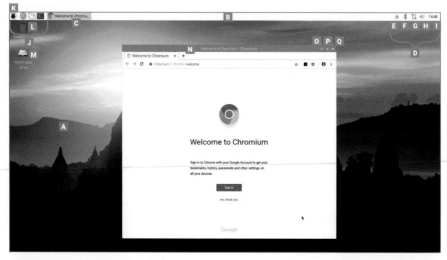

▲ **Figure 3-7:** The Raspbian desktop

A	Wallpaper	**G**	Network Icon	**M**	Removable Drive Icon
B	Taskbar	**H**	Volume Icon	**N**	Window Titlebar
C	Task	**I**	Clock	**O**	Minimise
D	System Tray	**J**	Launcher	**P**	Maximise
E	Media Eject	**K**	Menu (or Raspberry) Icon	**Q**	Close
F	Bluetooth Icon	**L**	Wastebasket Icon		

The right-hand side of the menu bar houses the *system tray* (**D**). If you have any *removable storage*, such as USB memory sticks, connected to Raspberry Pi you'll see an eject symbol (**E**); clicking on this will allow you to safely eject and remove them. On the far right is the clock (**I**); click on it to bring up a digital calendar (**Figure 3-8**).

▸ **Figure 3-8:** The digital calendar

Next to this is a speaker icon (**H**); click on it with the left mouse button to adjust Raspberry Pi's audio volume, or click using the right mouse button to choose which output Raspberry Pi should use. Next to that is a network icon (**G**); if you're connected to a wireless network you'll see the signal strength displayed as a series of bars, while if you're connected to a wired network you'll just see two arrows. Clicking the network icon will bring up a list of nearby wireless networks (**Figure 3-9**), while clicking on the Bluetooth icon (**F**) next to that will allow you to connect to a nearby Bluetooth device.

◀ **Figure 3-9:** Listing nearby wireless networks

The left-hand side of the menu bar is home to the *launcher* (**J**), which is where you'll find the programs installed alongside Raspbian. Some of these are visible as shortcut icons; others are hidden away in the menu, which you can bring up by clicking the raspberry icon (**K**) to the far left (**Figure 3-10**).

◀ **Figure 3-10:** The Raspbian menu

The programs in the menu are split into categories, the names of which tell you what to expect: the Programming category, for example, contains software designed to help you write your own programs – as explained starting in **Chapter 4, Programming with Scratch** – while Games will help you while away the hours. Not all of the programs will be detailed in this guide; feel free to experiment with them to learn more.

The Chromium web browser

To practise using your Raspberry Pi, start by loading the Chromium web browser: click on the raspberry icon at the top-left to bring up the menu, move your mouse pointer to select the Internet category, and click on Chromium Web Browser to load it (**Figure 3-11**).

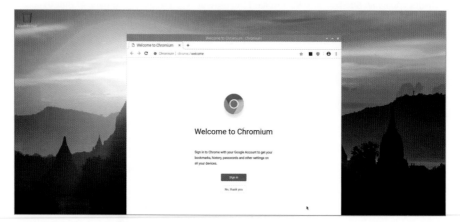

▲ **Figure 3-11:** The Chromium web browser

If you've used Google's Chrome browser on another computer, Chromium will be immediately familiar. As a web browser, Chromium lets you visit websites, play videos, games, and even communicate with people all over the world on forums and chat sites.

Start using Chromium by maximising its window so it takes up more of the screen: find the three icons at the top-right of the Chromium window titlebar (**N**) and click on the middle, up-arrow icon (**P**). This is the *maximise* button, and will make a window fill the screen. To the left of maximise is *minimise* (**O**), which will hide a window until you click on it in the taskbar at the top of the screen. The cross to the right of maximise is *close* (**Q**), and does exactly what you'd expect: closes the window.

CLOSE AND SAVE

Closing a window before you've saved any work you've done is a bad idea; while many programs will warn you to save when you click the close button, others won't.

Click in the address bar at the top of the Chromium window – the big white bar with a magnifying glass on the left-hand side – and type **www.raspberrypi.org**, then press the **ENTER** key on your keyboard. The Raspberry Pi website will load (**Figure 3-12**). You can also type searches into the address bar: try searching for 'Raspberry Pi', 'Raspbian', or 'Educational Computing'.

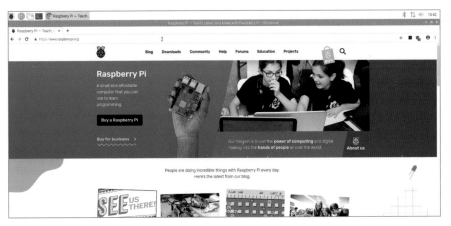

▲ **Figure 3-12:** Loading the Raspberry Pi website in Chromium

The first time you load Chromium, it may bring up several *tabs* along the top of the window. To switch to a different tab, click on it; to close a tab without closing Chromium itself, click the cross on the right-hand edge of the tab you want to close. To open a new tab, which is a handy way of having multiple websites open without having to juggle multiple Chromium windows, either click on the tab button to the right of the last tab in the list, or hold down the **CTRL** key on the keyboard and press the **T** key before letting go of **CTRL**.

When you're finished with Chromium, click the close button at the top-right of the window.

The File Manager

Files you save – whether they're programs or poems you've written, videos you've created, or images you've downloaded from a website – all go into your *home directory*. To see the home directory, click on the raspberry icon again to bring up the menu, move the mouse pointer to select Accessories, then click on File Manager to load it (**Figure 3-13**).

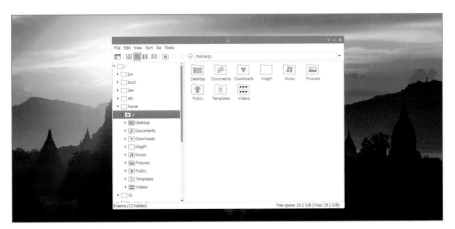

▲ **Figure 3-13:** The File Manager program

The File Manager lets you browse the files and folders, also known as *directories*, on Raspberry Pi's microSD card, as well as those on any removable storage devices – like USB flash drives – you connect to Raspberry Pi's USB ports. When you first open it, it automatically goes to your home directory. In here you'll find a series of other folders, known as *subdirectories*, which – like the menu – are arranged in categories. The main subdirectories are:

- **Desktop:** This folder is what you see when you first load Raspbian; if you save a file in here it will appear on the Raspbian desktop, making it easy to find and load.

- **Documents:** The Documents folder is home to most of the files you'll create, from short stories to recipes.

- **Downloads:** When you download a file from the internet using the Chromium web browser, it will be automatically saved in Downloads.

- **MagPi:** This folder contains an electronic copy of *The MagPi*, the official magazine of the Raspberry Pi Foundation.

- **Music:** Any music you create or put on Raspberry Pi can be stored here.

- **Pictures:** This folder is specifically for pictures, known in technical terms as *image files*.

- **Public:** While most of your files are private, anything you put in Public will be available to other users of Raspberry Pi, even if they have their own username and password.

- **Videos:** A folder for videos, and the first place most video-playing programs will look.

The File Manager window itself is split into two panes: the left pane shows the directories on your Raspberry Pi, and the right pane shows the files and subdirectories of the directory selected in the left pane. If you plug a removable storage device into Raspberry Pi's USB port, a window will pop up asking if you'd like to open it in the File Manager (**Figure 3-14**); click OK and you'll be able to see its files and directories.

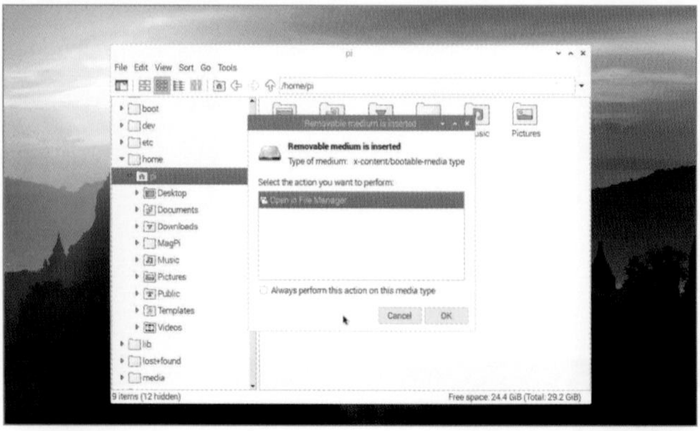

◀ Figure 3-14: Inserting a removable storage device

Files on a removable device can easily be copied to Raspberry Pi's microSD card, or from the microSD card to a removable device: with both your home directory and the removable device open in separate File Manager windows, move your mouse pointer to the file you want to copy, click and hold the left mouse button down, slide your mouse pointer to the other window, and let go of the mouse button (**Figure 3-15**). This is known as *dragging and dropping*.

Another method is to click once on the file, click on the Edit menu, click on Copy, click on the other window, click on the Edit menu, and click on Paste.

The Move option, also available in the Edit menu, is similar except it deletes the file from its original home after making the copy

Both options can also be used through the keyboard shortcuts **CTRL+C** (copy) or **CTRL+X** (cut), and paste via **CTRL+V**.

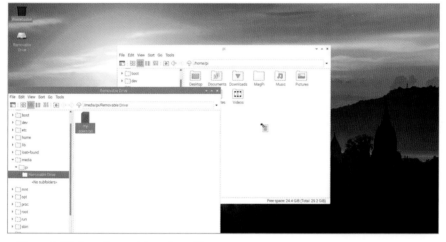

▲ **Figure 3-15:** Dragging and dropping a file

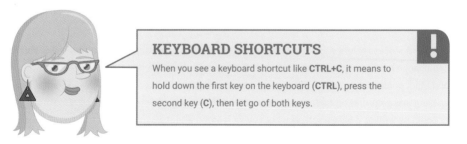

KEYBOARD SHORTCUTS

When you see a keyboard shortcut like **CTRL+C**, it means to hold down the first key on the keyboard (**CTRL**), press the second key (**C**), then let go of both keys.

When you've finished experimenting, close the File Manager by clicking the close button at the top-left of the window. If you have more than one window open, close them all. If you connected a removable storage device to your Raspberry Pi, eject it by clicking the eject button at the top-right of the screen, finding it in the list, and clicking on it before unplugging it.

The LibreOffice productivity suite

For another taste of what Raspberry Pi can do, click on the raspberry menu icon, move your
mouse pointer to Office, and click on LibreOffice Writer. This will load the word processor
portion of LibreOffice (**Figure 3-16**), a popular *productivity suite* – if you've used Microsoft
Office or Google Docs, you've used a productivity suite.

Note: LibreOffice may not be installed by default on all Raspbian OS images; if not, use the
Recommended Software tool (see page 42) to install it.

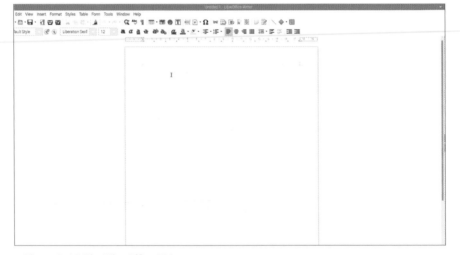

▲ **Figure 3-16:** The LibreOffice Writer program

A word processor lets you not only write documents, but to format them in clever ways: you
can change the font style, colour, size, add effects, and even insert pictures, charts, tables,
and other content. A word processor also lets you check your work for mistakes, highlighting
spelling and grammar problems in red and green respectively as you type.

Begin by writing a paragraph on what you've learned about Raspberry Pi and its software
so far. Experiment with the different icons at the top of the window to see what they do: see
if you can make your writing bigger, and change its colour. If you're not sure how to do this,
simply move your mouse pointer over each icon in turn to see a 'tool tip' telling you what that
icon does. When you're happy, click the File menu and the Save option to save your work
(**Figure 3-17**). Give it a name and click the Save button.

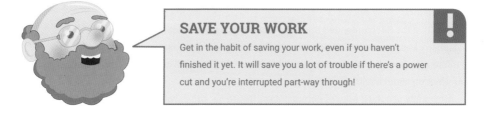

▲ **Figure 3-17:** Saving a document

SAVE YOUR WORK

Get in the habit of saving your work, even if you haven't finished it yet. It will save you a lot of trouble if there's a power cut and you're interrupted part-way through!

LibreOffice Writer is only part of the overall LibreOffice productivity suite. The other parts, which you'll find in the same Office menu category as LibreOffice Writer, are:

- **LibreOffice Base:** A database; a tool for storing information, looking it up quickly, and analysing it.

- **LibreOffice Calc**: A spreadsheet; a tool for handling numbers and creating charts and graphs.

- **LibreOffice Draw**: An illustration program; a tool for creating pictures and diagrams.

- **LibreOffice Impress**: A presentation program, for creating slides and running slideshows.

- **LibreOffice Math**: A formula editor; a tool for creating properly formatted mathematical formulae which can then be used in other documents.

LibreOffice is also available for other computers and operating systems. If you enjoy using it on your Raspberry Pi, you can download it for free from **libreoffice.org** and install it on any Microsoft Windows, Apple macOS, or Linux computer.

If you want to know more about using LibreOffice, click on the Help menu. Otherwise, close LibreOffice Writer by clicking the close button at the top-right of the window.

GETTING HELP

Most programs include a Help menu which has everything from information about what the program is to guides on how to use it. If you ever feel lost or overwhelmed by a program, look for the Help menu to reorient yourself.

The Recommended Software tool

Although Raspbian comes preloaded with a wide range of software, it's compatible with even more. A selection of the best of this software can be found in the Recommended Software tool.

Note that the Recommended Software tool needs a connection to the internet. If your Raspberry Pi is connected, click on the raspberry menu icon, move your mouse pointer to Preferences, and click on Recommended Software. The tool will load, then begin downloading information about available software.

After a few seconds, a list of compatible software packages will appear (**Figure 3-18**). These, like the software in the raspberry menu, are arranged into various categories. Click on a category in the pane on the left to see software from that category, or click All Programs to see everything.

▲ **Figure 3-18:** The Recommended Software tool

If a piece of software has a tick next to it, it's already installed on your Raspberry Pi. If it doesn't, you can click on the check-box next to it to add a tick and mark it for installation. You can mark as many pieces of software as you like before installing them all at once, but if you're using a smaller than recommended microSD card you may not have room for them all.

You can also uninstall software in the same way: find a piece of software which already has a tick in its check box, then click on the tick to remove it. If you've made a mistake or changed your mind, just click again to put the tick back.

When you're happy with your software selection, click the OK button to begin the installation or uninstallation process (**Figure 3-19**). After downloading and installing any new software you've chosen, a dialogue box will appear; click OK to close the Recommended Software tool.

▲ **Figure 3-19:** Uninstalling software

An additional tool for installing or uninstalling software, the Add/Remove Software tool, can be found in the same Preferences category of the Raspbian menu. This offers a wider selection of software, but which has not been vetted by the Raspberry Pi Foundation.

Raspberry Pi Configuration tool

The last program you'll learn about in this chapter is known as the Raspberry Pi Configuration tool, and it's a lot like the Welcome Wizard you used at the start: it allows you to change various settings in Raspbian. Click on the raspberry icon, move your mouse pointer to select the Preferences category, then click on Raspberry Pi Configuration to load it (**Figure 3-20**).

◄ **Figure 3-20:**
The Raspberry Pi
Configuration tool

The tool is split into five tabs. The first of these is System: this allows you to change the password of your account, set a host name – the name Raspberry Pi uses on your local wireless or wired network – and alter a range of other settings. The majority of these, though, shouldn't need changing. Click on the Display tab to bring up the next category. Here you can alter the screen display settings if needed, to suit your TV or monitor.

> **MORE DETAILS**
>
> This brief overview is simply to get you used to the tool. More detailed information on each of its settings can be found in **Appendix E, The Raspberry Pi Configuration Tool**.

The Interface tab offers a range of settings, all of which start off disabled. These settings should only be changed if you're adding new hardware, such as the Raspberry Pi Camera Module, and then only if instructed by the hardware's manufacturer. The exceptions to this rule are: SSH, which enables a 'Secure Shell' and lets you log into Raspberry Pi from another computer on your network using an SSH client; VNC, which enables a 'Virtual Network Computer' and lets you see and control the Raspbian desktop from another computer on your network using a VNC client; and Remote GPIO, which lets you use Raspberry Pi's GPIO pins

– about which you'll learn more in **Chapter 6, Physical computing with Scratch and Python** – from another computer on your network.

Click on the Performance tab to see the fourth category. Here you can set the amount of memory used by Raspberry Pi's graphics processing unit (GPU) and, for some models, increase the performance of Raspberry Pi through a process known as *overclocking*. As before, though, it's best to leave these settings alone unless you know you need to change them.

Finally, click on the Localisation tab to see the last category. Here you can change your locale, which controls things like the language used in Raspbian and how numbers are displayed, change the time zone, change the keyboard layout, and set your country for WiFi purposes. For now, though, just click on Cancel to close the tool without making any changes.

WARNING!

Different countries have different rules about what frequencies a WiFi radio can use. Setting the WiFi country in the Raspberry Pi Configuration Tool to a different country from the one you're actually in is likely to make it struggle to connect to your networks and can even be illegal under radio licensing laws – so don't do it!

Shutting down

Now you've explored the Raspbian desktop, it's time to learn a very important skill: safely shutting your Raspberry Pi down. Like any computer, Raspberry Pi keeps the files you're working on in *volatile memory* – memory which is emptied when the system is switched off. For documents you're creating, it's enough to save each in turn – which takes the file from volatile memory to *non-volatile memory*, the microSD card – to ensure you don't lose anything.

The documents you're working on aren't the only files open, though. Raspbian itself keeps a number of files open while it's running, and pulling the power cable from your Raspberry Pi while these are still open can result in the operating system becoming corrupt and needing to be reinstalled.

To prevent this from happening, you need to make sure you tell Raspbian to save all its files and make itself ready for being powered off – a process known as *shutting down* the operating system.

WARNING!

Never pull the power cable from a Raspberry Pi without shutting it down first. Doing so is likely to corrupt the operating system and could also lose any files you have created or downloaded.

Click on the raspberry icon at the top left of the desktop and then click on Shutdown. A window will appear with three options (**Figure 3-21**): Shutdown, Reboot, and Logout. Shutdown is the option you'll use most: clicking on this will tell Raspbian to close all open software and files, then shut Raspberry Pi down. Once the display has gone black, wait a few seconds until the flashing green light on Raspberry Pi goes off; then it's safe to turn off the power supply.

To turn Raspberry Pi back on, simply disconnect then reconnect the power cable, or toggle the power at the wall socket.

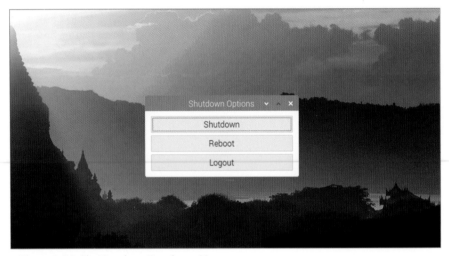

▲ **Figure 3-21:** Shutting down Raspberry Pi

Reboot goes through a similar process to Shutdown, closing everything down, but instead of turning Raspberry Pi's power off, it restarts Raspberry Pi – in almost exactly the same way as if you'd chosen Shutdown, then disconnected and reconnected the power cable. You'll need to use Reboot if you make certain changes which require a restart of the operating system – such as installing certain updates to its core software – or if some software has gone wrong, known as *crashing*, and left Raspbian in an unusable state.

Finally, Logout is only really useful if you have more than one user account on your Raspberry Pi: it closes any programs you currently have open and takes you to a login screen on which you are prompted for a username and password. If you hit Logout by mistake and want to get back in, simply type 'pi' as the username and whatever password you chose in the Welcome Wizard at the start of this chapter.

Chapter 4

Programming with Scratch 3

Learn how to start coding using Scratch, the block-based programming language

Using Raspberry Pi isn't just about using software other people have created; it's about creating your own software, based on almost anything your imagination can conjure. Whether you have previous experience with creating your own programs – a process known as programming or coding – or not, you'll find Raspberry Pi a great platform for creation and experimentation.

Key to the accessibility of coding on Raspberry Pi is Scratch, a visual programming language developed by the Massachusetts Institute of Technology (MIT). Whereas traditional programming languages have you write text-based instructions for the computer to carry out, in much the same way as you might write a recipe for baking a cake, Scratch has you build your program step-by-step using blocks – pre-written chunks of code hidden behind colour-coded jigsaw pieces.

Scratch is a great first language for budding coders young and old, but don't be fooled by its friendly appearance: it's a powerful and fully functional programming environment for creating everything from simple games and animations through to complex interactive robotics projects.

Introducing the Scratch 3 interface

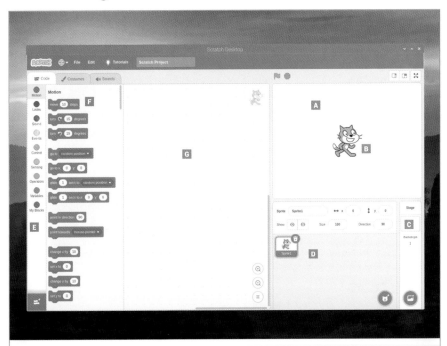

A **Stage Area** – Like actors in a play, your sprites move around the stage under the control of your program.

B **Sprite** – The characters or objects you control in a Scratch program are known as sprites, and sit on the stage.

C **Stage Controls** – Your stage can be changed, including adding your own pictures as backgrounds, using the stage controls.

D **Sprites List** – All the sprites you have created or loaded into Scratch will appear in this section of the window.

E **Blocks Palette** – All the blocks available for your program appear in the blocks palette, which features colour-coded categories.

SCRATCH VERSIONS

At the time of writing, Raspbian comes with three versions of Scratch: 1, 2 and 3, all included in the Programming section of the menu. This chapter is written for Scratch 3, which will only run on Raspberry Pi 4. Scratch 1 runs on all models; Scratch 2 on Raspberry 2 onwards. Scratch 2 versions of the three main projects in this chapter may be found via the weblinks provided.

F **Blocks** – Pre-written chunks of program code, blocks allow you to build your program step-by-step.

G **Code Area** – The code area is where your program is built by dragging-and-dropping blocks from the blocks palette to form scripts.

Your first Scratch program: Hello, World!

Scratch 3 loads like any other program on Raspberry Pi: click on the raspberry icon to load the Raspbian menu, move the cursor to the Programming section, and click on Scratch 3. After a few seconds, the Scratch 3 user interface will load.

Where most programming languages need you to tell the computer what to do through written instructions, Scratch is different. Start by clicking on the Looks category in the blocks palette, found at the left of the Scratch window. This brings up the blocks under that category, coloured purple. Find the **say Hello!** block, click and hold the left mouse button on it, and drag it over to the code area at the centre of the Scratch window before letting go of the mouse button (**Figure 4-1**).

▲ **Figure 4-1:** Drag and drop the block into the code area

Look at the shape of the block you've just dropped: it has a hole at the top, and a matching part sticking out at the bottom. Like a jigsaw piece, this shows you that the block is expecting to have something above it and something below it. For this program, that something above is a *trigger*.

Click on the Events category of the blocks palette, coloured gold, then click and drag the **when ⚑ clicked** block – known as a *hat* block – onto the code area. Position it so that the bit sticking out of the bottom connects into the hole at the top of your **say Hello!** block until you see a white outline, then let go of the mouse button. You don't have to be precise; if it's close enough, the block will snap into place just like a jigsaw piece. If it doesn't, click and hold on it again to adjust its position until it does.

Your program is now complete. To make it work, known as *running* the program, click on the green flag icon at the top-left of the stage area. If all has gone well, the cat sprite on the stage will greet you with a cheery 'Hello!' (**Figure 4-2**) – your first program is a success!

▲ **Figure 4-2:** Click the green flag above the stage and the cat will say 'Hello'

Before moving on, name and save your program. Click on the File menu, then 'Save to your computer'. Type in a name and click the Save button (**Figure 4-3**).

▲ **Figure 4-3:** Save your program with a memorable name

WHAT CAN IT SAY?

Some blocks in Scratch can be changed. Try clicking on the word 'Hello!' and typing something else, then click the green flag again. What happens on the stage?

Next steps: sequencing

While your program has two blocks, it only has one real instruction: to say 'Hello!' every time the flag is clicked and the program runs. To do more, you need to know about *sequencing*. Computer programs, at their simplest, are a list of instructions, just like a recipe. Each instruction follows on from the last in a logical progression known as a *linear sequence*.

Start by clicking and dragging the `say Hello!` block from the code area back to the blocks palette (**Figure 4-4**). This deletes the block, removing it from your program and leaving just the trigger block, `when ⚑ clicked`.

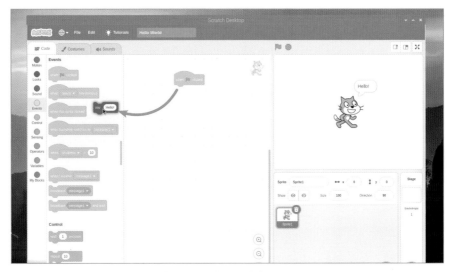

▲ **Figure 4-4:** To delete a block, simply drag it out of the code area

Click on the Motion category in the blocks palette, then click and drag the move 10 steps block so it locks into place under the trigger block on the code area. As the name suggests, this tells your sprite – the cat – to move a number of steps in the direction it's currently facing.

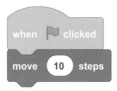

Add more instructions to your program to create a sequence. Click on the Sound palette, colour-coded pink, then click and drag the play sound Meow until done block so it locks underneath the move 10 steps block. Keep going: click back on the Motion category and drag another move 10 steps block underneath your Sound block, but this time click on the '10' to select it and type '-10' to create a move -10 steps block.

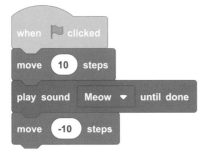

Click on the green flag above the stage to run the program. You'll see the cat move to the right, make a meow sound — make sure you've got speakers or headphones connected to hear it — then move back to the start again. Click the flag again, and the cat will repeat its actions.

Congratulations: you've created a sequence of instructions, which Scratch is running through one at a time, top to bottom. While Scratch will only run one instruction at a time from the sequence, it does so very quickly: try deleting the **play sound Meow until done** block by clicking and dragging the bottom **move -10 steps** block to detach it, dragging the **play sound Meow until done** block to the blocks palette, then replacing it with the simpler **play sound Meow** block before dragging your **move -10 steps** block back onto the bottom of your program.

Click the green flag to run your program again, and the cat sprite doesn't seem to move. The sprite is moving, in fact, but it moves back again so quickly that it appears to be standing still. This is because using the **play sound Meow** block doesn't wait for the sound to finish playing before the next step; because Raspberry Pi 'thinks' so quickly, the next instruction runs before you can ever see the cat sprite move. There's another way to fix this, beyond using the **play sound Meow until done** block: click on the light orange Control category of the blocks palette, then click and drag a **wait 1 seconds** block between the **play sound Meow** block and the bottom **move -10 steps** block.

Click the green flag to run your program one last time, and you'll see that the cat sprite waits for a second after moving to the right before moving back to the left again. This is known as a *delay*, and is key to controlling how long your sequence of instructions takes to run.

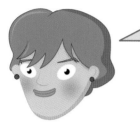

CHALLENGE: ADD MORE STEPS

Try adding more steps to your sequence, and changing the values in the existing steps. What happens when the number of steps in one move block doesn't match the number of steps in another? What happens if you try to play a sound while another sound is still playing?

Looping the loop

The sequence you've created so far runs only once: you click the green flag, the cat sprite moves and meows, and then the program stops until you click the green flag again. It doesn't have to stop, though, because Scratch includes a type of Control block known as a *loop*.

Click on the Control category in the blocks palette and find the forever block. Click and drag this into the code area, then drop it underneath the when ⚑ clicked block and above the first move 10 steps block.

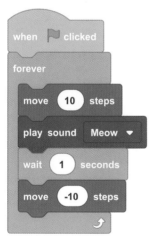

Notice how the C-shaped forever block automatically grows to surround the other blocks in your sequence. Click the green flag now, and you'll quickly see what the forever block does: instead of your program running once and finishing, it will run over and over again – quite literally forever. In programming, this is known as an *infinite loop* – literally, a loop that never ends.

If the sound of constant meowing is getting a little much, click the red octagon next to the green flag above the stage area to stop your program. To change the loop type, click and drag the first move 10 steps block and pull it and the blocks beneath it out of the forever block, then drop them underneath the when 🏳 clicked block. Click and drag the forever block to the blocks palette to delete it, then click and drag the repeat 10 block under the when 🏳 clicked block so it goes around the other blocks.

Click the green flag to run your new program. At first, it seems to be doing the same thing as your original version: repeating your sequence of instructions over and over again. This time, though, rather than continuing forever, the loop will finish after ten repetitions. This is known as a *definite loop*: you define when it will finish. Loops are powerful tools, and most programs – especially games and sensing programs – make heavy use of both infinite and definite loops.

WHAT HAPPENS NOW?
What happens if you change the number in the loop block to make it larger? What happens if it's smaller? What happens if you put the number 0 in the loop block?

Variables and conditionals

The final concepts to understand before beginning to code Scratch programs in earnest are closely related: *variables* and *conditionals*. A variable is, as the name suggests, a value which can vary – in other words, change – over time and under control of the program. A variable has two main properties: its name, and the value it stores. That value doesn't have to be a number, either: it can be numbers, text, true-or-false, or completely empty – known as a *null value*.

Variables are powerful tools. Think of the things you have to track in a game: the health of a character, the speed of moving object, the level currently being played, and the score. All of these are tracked as variables.

First, click the File menu and save your existing program by clicking on 'Save to your computer'. If you already saved the program earlier, you'll be asked if you want to overwrite it, replacing the old saved copy with your new up-to-date version. Next, click File and then New to start a new, blank project (click OK when asked if you want to replace the contents of the current project). Click on the dark orange Variables category in the blocks palette, then the 'Make a Variable' button. Type 'loops' as the variable name (**Figure 4-5**), then click OK to make a series of blocks appear in the blocks palette.

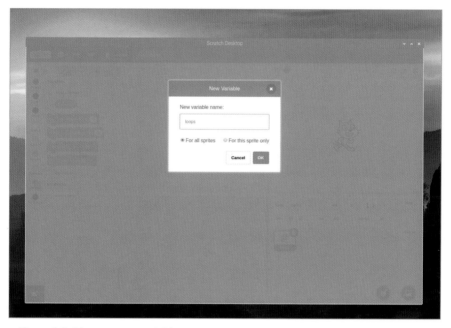

▲ **Figure 4-5:** Give your new variable a name

Click and drag the set loops to 0 block to the code area. This tells your program to *initialise* the variable with a value of 0. Next, click on the Looks category of the blocks palette and drag the say Hello! for 2 seconds block under your set loops to 0 block.

As you found earlier, the say Hello! blocks cause the cat sprite to say whatever is written in them. Rather than writing the message in the block yourself, though, you can use a variable instead. Click back onto the Variables category in the blocks palette, then click and drag the rounded loops block – known as a *reporter block* and found at the top of the list, with a tick-box next to it – over the word 'Hello!' in your  block. This creates a new, combined block: say loops for 2 seconds .

set loops ▼ to 0

say loops for 2 seconds

Click on the Events category in the blocks palette, then click and drag the when 🏳 clicked block to place it on top of your sequence of blocks. Click the green flag above the stage area, and you'll see the cat sprite say '0' (**Figure 4-6**) – the value you gave to the variable 'loops'.

▲ **Figure 4-6:** This time the cat will say the value of the variable

Variables aren't unchanging, though. Click on the Variables category in the blocks palette, then click and drag the change loops by 1 block to the bottom of your sequence. Next, click on the Control category, then click and drag a repeat 10 block and drop it so that it starts directly beneath your set loops to 0 block and wraps around the remaining blocks in your sequence.

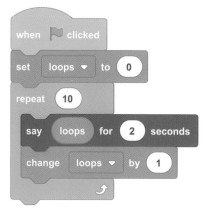

Click the green flag again. This time, you'll see the cat count upwards from 0 to 9. This works because your program is now changing, or *modifying*, the variable itself: every time the loop runs, the program adds one to the value in the 'loops' variable (**Figure 4-7**).

▲ **Figure 4-7:** Thanks to the loop, the cat now counts upwards

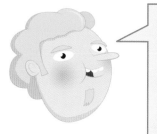

COUNTING FROM ZERO

Although the loop you've created runs ten times, the cat sprite only counts up to nine. This is because we're starting with a value of zero for our variable. Including zero and nine, there are ten numbers between zero and nine – so the program stops before the cat ever says '10'. To change this you could set the variable's initial value to 1 instead of 0.

You can do more with a variable than modify it. Click and drag the say loops for 2 seconds block to break it out of the repeat 10 block and drop it below the repeat 10 block. Click and drag the repeat 10 block to the blocks palette to delete it, then replace it with a repeat until block, making sure the block is connected to the bottom of the say loops for 2 seconds block and surrounds both of the other blocks in your sequence. Click on the Operators category in the blocks palette, colour-coded green, then click and drag the diamond-shaped ◯=◯ block and drop it on the matching diamond-shaped hole in the repeat until block.

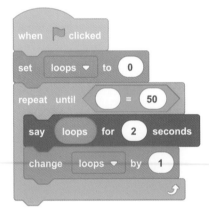

This Operators block lets you compare two values, including variables. Click on the Variables category, drag the loops reporter block into the empty space in the ◯=◯ Operators block, then click on the space with '50' in it and type the number '10'.

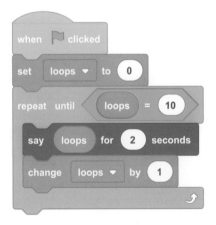

Click on the green flag above the stage area, and you'll find the program works the same way as before: the cat sprite counts from 0 up to 9 (**Figure 4-8**) and then the program stops.

This is because the `repeat until` block is working in exactly the same way as the `repeat 10` block, but rather than counting the number of loops itself, it's comparing the value of the 'loops' variable to the value you typed to the right of the block. When the 'loops' variable reaches 10, the program stops.

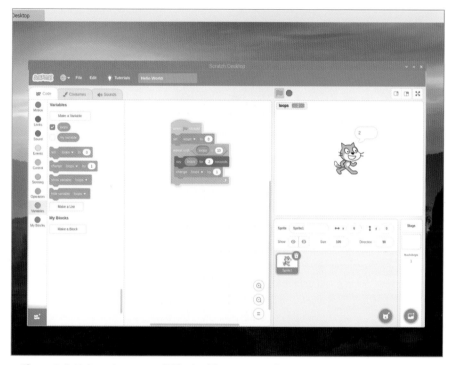

▲ **Figure 4-8:** Using a 'repeat until' block with a comparative operator

This is known as a *comparative operator*: it literally compares two values. Click on the Operators category of the blocks palette, and find the two other diamond-shape blocks above and below the one with the '=' symbol. These are also comparative operators: '<' compares two values and is triggered when the value of the left is smaller than the one on the right, and '>' triggers when the value on the left is bigger than the one on the right.

Click on the Control category of the blocks palette, find the `if then` block, then click and drag it to the code area before dropping it directly beneath the `say loops for 2 seconds` block. It will automatically surround the `change loops by 1` block, so click and drag on that to move it so it connects to the bottom of your `if then` block instead. Click on the Looks category of the blocks palette, then click and drag a `say Hello! for 2 seconds` block to drop it inside your `if then` block. Click on the Operators category of the blocks palette, then click and drag the `< > >` block into the diamond-shape hole in your `if then` block.

The if then block is a conditional block, which means the blocks inside it will only run if a certain condition is met. Click on the Variables category of the blocks palette, drag and drop the loops reporter block into the empty space in your ○>○ block, then click on the space with '50' in it and type the number '5'. Finally, click on the word 'Hello!' in your say Hello! for 2 seconds block and type 'That's high!'.

Click on the green flag. At first, the program will work as before with the cat sprite counting upwards from zero. When the number reaches 6, the first number which is greater than 5, the `if then` block will begin to trigger and the cat sprite will comment on how high the numbers are getting (**Figure 4-9**). Congratulations: you can now work with variables and conditionals!

▲ **Figure 4-9:** The cat makes a comment when the number reaches 6

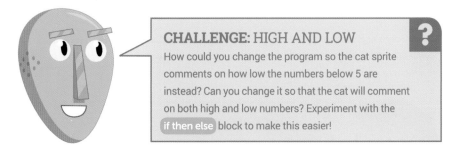

CHALLENGE: HIGH AND LOW
How could you change the program so the cat sprite comments on how low the numbers below 5 are instead? Can you change it so that the cat will comment on both high and low numbers? Experiment with the `if then else` block to make this easier!

Project 1: **Astronaut Reaction Timer**

Now you understand how Scratch works, it's time to make something a little more interactive: a reaction timer, designed to honour British ESA astronaut Tim Peake and his time aboard the International Space Station.

ONLINE PROJECT
A Scratch 2 version of this project is available online at **rpf.io/astronaut-game**

Save your existing program, if you want to keep it, then open a new project by clicking on File and New. Before you begin, give it a name by clicking on File and 'Save to your computer': call it 'Astronaut Reaction Timer'.

This project relies on two images – one as a stage background, one as a sprite – which are not included in Scratch's built-in resources. To download them, click on the raspberry icon to load the Raspbian menu, move the mouse pointer to Internet, and click on Chromium Web Browser. When the browser has loaded, type **rpf.io/astronaut-backdrop** into the address bar, followed by the **ENTER** key. Right-click on the picture of space and click on 'Save image as…', then click on the Save button (**Figure 4-10**). Click back into the address bar, and type **rpf.io/astronaut-sprite** followed by the **ENTER** key.

▲ **Figure 4-10:** Save the background image

Again, right-click on the picture of Tim Peake and click on 'Save image as…', then choose the Downloads folder and click on the Save button. With those two images saved, you can close Chromium or leave it open and use the taskbar to switch back to Scratch 3.

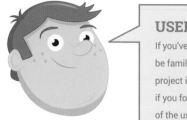

USER INTERFACE

If you've been following this chapter from the start, you should be familiar with the Scratch 3 user interface. The following project instructions will rely on you knowing where things are; if you forget where to find something, look back at the picture of the user interface at the start of this chapter for a reminder.

Right-click the cat sprite in the list and click 'delete'. Hover the mouse pointer over the Choose a Backdrop icon 🖼, then click the Upload Backdrop icon 🔼 from the list that appears. Find the **Space-background.png** file in the Downloads folder, click on it to select it, then click OK. The plain white stage background will change to the picture of space, and the code area will be replaced by the backdrops area (**Figure 4-11**). Here you can draw over the backdrop, but for now just click on the tab marked Code at the top of the Scratch 3 window.

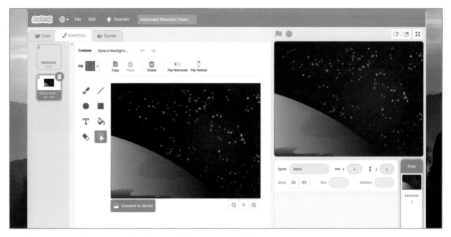

▲ **Figure 4-11:** The space background appears on the stage

Upload your new sprite by hovering your mouse pointer over the Choose a Sprite icon 👾, then clicking on the Upload Sprite icon 📤 at the top of the list that appears. Find the file **Astronaut-Tim.png** in the Downloads folder, click to select it, then click OK. The sprite appears on the stage automatically, but might not be in the middle: click and drag it with the mouse and drop it so it's near the lower middle (**Figure 4-12**).

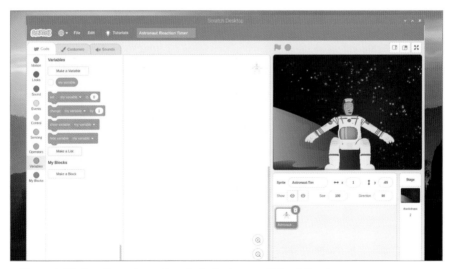

▲ **Figure 4-12:** Drag the astronaut sprite to the lower middle of the stage

With your new background and sprite in place, you're ready to create your program. Start by creating a new variable called 'time', making sure that 'For all sprites' is selected before clicking OK. Click on your sprite – either on the stage or in the sprite pane – to select it, then add a  when ⚑ clicked block from the Events category to the code area. Next, add a say Hello! for 2 seconds block from the Looks category, then click on it to change it to say 'Hello! British ESA Astronaut Tim Peake here. Are you ready?'

when ⚑ clicked

say (Hello! British ESA Astronaut Tim Peake here. Are you ready?) for (2) seconds

Add a wait 1 seconds block from the Control category, then a say Hello! block. Change this block to say 'Hit Space!', then add a reset timer block from the Sensing category. This controls a special variable built into Scratch for timing things, and will be used to time how quickly you can react in the game.

when ⚑ clicked

say (Hello! British ESA Astronaut Tim Peake here. Are you ready?) for (2) seconds

wait (1) seconds

say (Hit Space!)

reset timer

Add a wait until Control block, then drag a key space pressed? Sensing block into its white space. This will pause the program until you press the **SPACE** key on the keyboard, but the timer will continue to run – counting exactly how long between the message telling you to 'Hit Space!' and you actually hitting the **SPACE** key.

when ⚑ clicked

say (Hello! British ESA Astronaut Tim Peake here. Are you ready?) for (2) seconds

wait (1) seconds

say (Hit Space!)

reset timer

wait until ⟨ key (space ▼) pressed? ⟩

You now need Tim to tell you how long you took to press the **SPACE** key, but in a way that's easy to read. To do this, you'll need a join Operators block. This takes two values, including variables, and joins them together one after the other – known as *concatenation*.

Start with a say Hello! block, then drag and drop a join Operators block over the word 'Hello!'. Click on 'apple' and type 'Your reaction time was ', making sure to add a blank space at the end, then drag another join block over the top of 'banana' in the second box. Drag a timer reporting block from the Sensing category into what is now the middle box, and type ' seconds.' into the last box – making sure to include a blank space at the start.

```
when 🏴 clicked
say  Hello! British ESA Astronaut Tim Peake here. Are you ready?   for  2  seconds
wait  1  seconds
say  Hit Space!
reset  timer
wait until  key  space ▼  pressed?
say  join  Your reaction time was   join  timer   seconds
```

Finally, drag a set my variable to 0 Variables block onto the end of your sequence. Click on the drop-down arrow next to 'my variable' and click on 'time' from the list, then replace the '0' with a timer reporting block from the Sensing category. Your game is now ready to test by clicking on the green flag above the stage. Get ready, and as soon as you see the message 'Hit Space!', press the **SPACE** key as quickly as you can (**Figure 4-13**) – see if you can beat our high score!

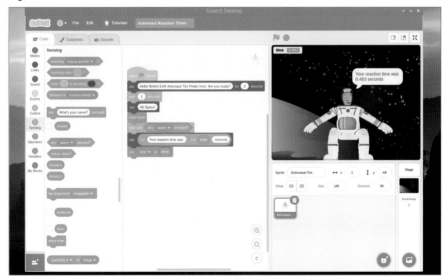

▲ **Figure 4-13:** Time to play the game!

You can extend this project further by having it calculate roughly how far the International Space Station has travelled in the time it took you to press the **SPACE** key, based on the station's published speed of seven kilometres per second. First, create a new variable called 'distance'. Notice how the blocks in the Variables category automatically change to show the new variable, but the existing time variable blocks in your program remain the same.

Add a set distance to 0 block, then drag a ● * ● Operators block – indicating multiplication – over the '0'. Drag a time reporting block over the first blank space, then type in the number '7' into the second space. When you're finished, your combined block reads set distance to time * 7 . This will take the time it took you to press the **SPACE** key and multiply it by seven, to get the distance in kilometres the ISS has travelled.

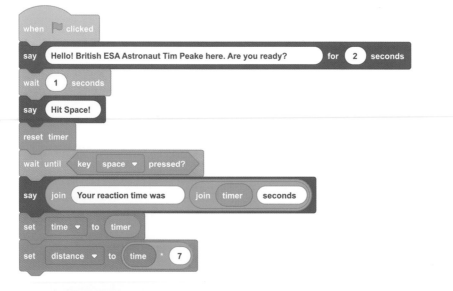

Add a wait 1 seconds block and change it '4'. Finally, drag another say Hello! block onto the end of your sequence and add two join blocks, just as you did before. In the first space, over 'apple' type 'In that time the ISS travels around ', remembering to include the space at the end; in the 'banana' space, type ' kilometres.', again remembering the space at the start.

```
when [flag] clicked
say [Hello! British ESA Astronaut Tim Peake here. Are you ready?] for (2) seconds
wait (1) seconds
say [Hit Space!]
reset timer
wait until <key (space ▼) pressed?>
say (join [Your reaction time was] (join (timer) [seconds]))
set (time ▼) to (timer)
set (distance ▼) to ((time) * (7))
wait (4) seconds
say (join [In that time the ISS travels around] (join (apple) [kilometres.]))
```

Finally, drag a `round` Operators block into the middle blank space, then drag a `distance` reporting block into the new blank space it creates. The `round` block rounds numbers up or down to their nearest whole number, so instead of a hyper-accurate but hard-to-read number of kilometres you'll get an easy-to-read whole number.

```
when [flag] clicked
say [Hello! British ESA Astronaut Tim Peake here. Are you ready?] for (2) seconds
wait (1) seconds
say [Hit Space!]
reset timer
wait until <key (space ▼) pressed?>
say (join [Your reaction time was] (join (timer) [seconds]))
set (time ▼) to (timer)
set (distance ▼) to ((time) * (7))
wait (4) seconds
say (join [In that time the ISS travels around] (join (round (distance)) [kilometres.]))
```

Click the green flag to run your program, and see how far the ISS travels in the time it takes you to hit the **SPACE** key. Remember to save your program when you've finished, so you can easily load it again in the future without having to start from the beginning!

▲ **Figure 4-14:** Tim tells you how far the ISS has travelled

CHALLENGE: WHO'S FAST?
As well as astronaut, what other professions require split-second reflexes? Can you draw your own sprites and backgrounds to show one of these professions?

Project 2: **Synchronised Swimming**

Most games use more than a single button, and this project demonstrates that by offering two-button control using the ← and → keys on the keyboard.

ONLINE PROJECT
This project is also available online at **rpf.io/synchro-swimming**

Create a new project and save it as 'Synchronised Swimming'. Click on the Stage in the stage control section, then click the Backdrops tab at the top-left. Click the Convert to Bitmap button below the backdrop. Choose a water-like blue colour from the Fill palette, click on the Fill icon 🎨, and then click on the chequered backdrop to fill it with blue (**Figure 4-15**).

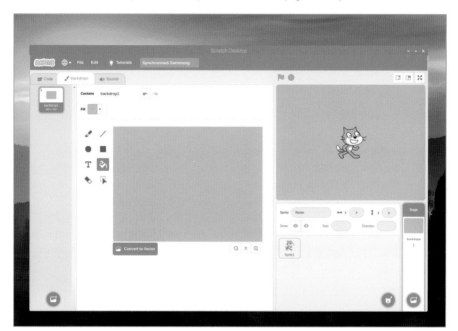

▲ **Figure 4-15:** Fill the background with a blue colour

Right-click the cat sprite in the list and click 'delete'. Click the 'Choose a Sprite' icon 🐱 to see a list of built-in sprites. Click on the Animals category, then 'Cat Flying' (**Figure 4-16**), then OK. This sprite also serves well for swimming projects.

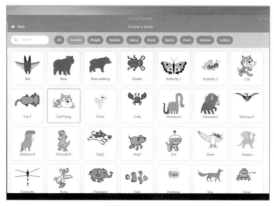

▲ **Figure 4-16:** Choose a sprite from the library

Click the new sprite, then drag two **when space key pressed** Events blocks into the code area. Click on the small down-arrow next to the word 'space' on the first block and choose 'left arrow' from the list of possible options. Drag a **turn ↻ 15 degrees** Motion block under your **when left arrow pressed** block, then do the same with your

second Events block except choosing 'right arrow' from the list and using a
turn C 15 degrees Motion block.

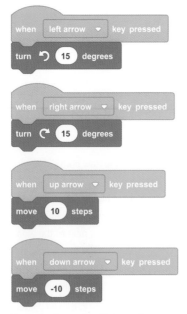

Press the ← or → key to test your program. You'll see the cat sprite turning as you do, matching the direction you're choosing on the keyboard. Notice how you didn't need to click on the green flag this time; this is because the Events trigger blocks you have used are active at all times, even when the program isn't 'running' in the normal sense.

Do the same steps twice again, but this time choosing 'up arrow' and 'down arrow' for the Events trigger blocks, then move 10 steps and move -10 steps for the Motion blocks. Press the arrow keys now and you'll see your cat can turn around and swim forwards and backwards too!

To make the cat sprite's motion more realistic, you can change how it appears – known in Scratch terms as its *costume*. Click on the cat sprite, then click on the Costumes tab above the blocks palette. Click on the 'cat flying-a' costume and click on the X-in-a-bin icon 🗑 that appears at its top-right corner to delete it. Next, click on the 'cat flying-b' costume and use the name box at the top to rename it to 'right' (**Figure 4-17**).

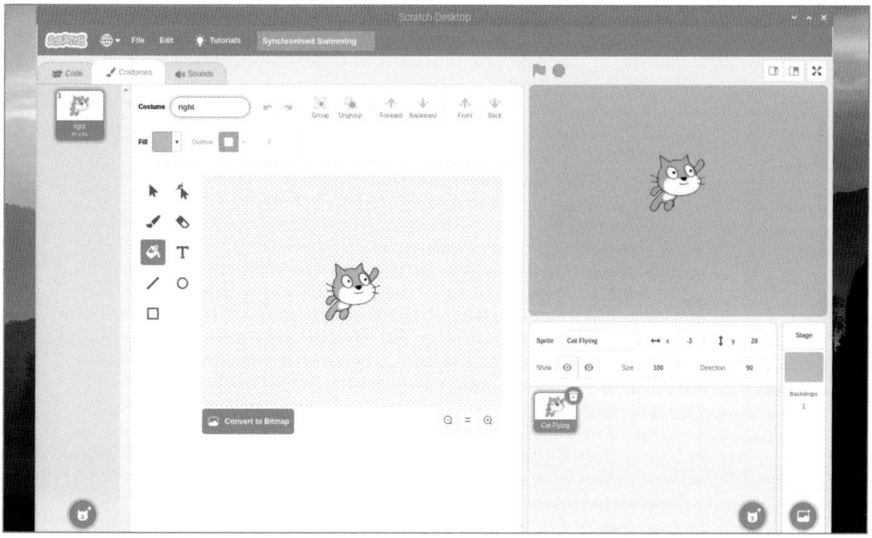

▲ **Figure 4-17:** Rename the costume as 'right'

Right-click on the newly renamed 'right' costume and click 'duplicate' to create a copy. Click on this copy to select it, click the Select icon ▶, click Flip Horizontal ▶◀, then rename it to 'left' (**Figure 4-18**). You'll finish with two 'costumes' for your sprite, which are exact mirror images: one called 'right' with the cat facing right, and one called 'left' with the cat facing left.

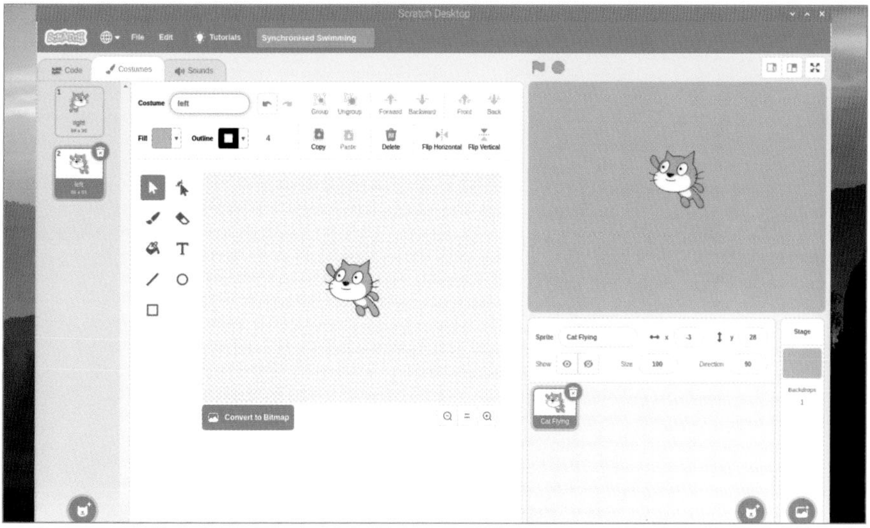

▲ **Figure 4-18:** Duplicate the costume, flip it, and name it 'left'

Click on the Code tab above the costume area, then drag two `switch costume to left` Looks blocks under your left arrow and right arrow Events blocks, changing the one under the right arrow block to read `switch costume to right`. Try the arrow keys again; the cat now seems to turn to face the direction it's swimming.

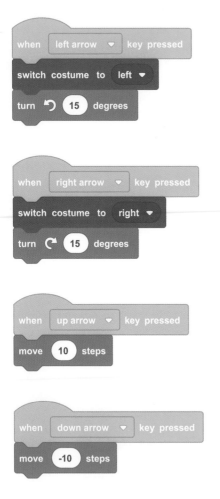

For Olympic-style synchronised swimming, though, we need more swimmers, and we need a way to reset the cat sprite's position. Add a when ⚑ clicked Events block, then underneath add a go to x: 0 y: 0 Motion block – changing the values if necessary – and a point in direction 90 Motion block. Now, when you click the green flag, the cat will be moved to the middle of the stage and pointing to the right.

```
when  left arrow  ▼  key pressed
switch costume to  left ▼
turn ↺ 15 degrees
```

```
when  right arrow  ▼  key pressed
switch costume to  right ▼
turn ↻ 15 degrees
```

```
when  up arrow  ▼  key pressed
move 10 steps
```

```
when  down arrow  ▼  key pressed
move -10 steps
```

```
when ⚑ clicked
go to x: 0 y: 0
point in direction 90
```

To create more swimmers, add a `repeat 6` block – changing from the default value of '10' – and add a `create clone of myself` Control block inside it. To make it so the swimmers aren't all swimming in the same direction, add a `turn C 60 degrees` block above the `create clone` block but still inside the `repeat 6` block. Click the green flag, and try the arrow keys now to see your swimmers come to life!

```
when  left arrow ▼  key pressed
switch costume to  left ▼
turn  ↺  15  degrees
```

```
when  right arrow ▼  key pressed
switch costume to  right ▼
turn  C  15  degrees
```

```
when  up arrow ▼  key pressed
move  10  steps
```

```
when  down arrow ▼  key pressed
move  -10  steps
```

```
when  ⚑ clicked
go to x:  0  y:  0
point in direction  90
repeat  6
    turn  C  60  degrees
    create clone of  myself ▼
```

To complete the Olympic feel, you'll need to add some music. Click on the Sounds tab above the blocks palette, then click the 'Choose a Sound' icon 🔊. Click on the Loops category, then browse through the list (**Figure 4-19**) until you find some music you like – we've picked 'Dance Around'. Click on the OK button to choose the music, then click on the Code tab to open the code area again.

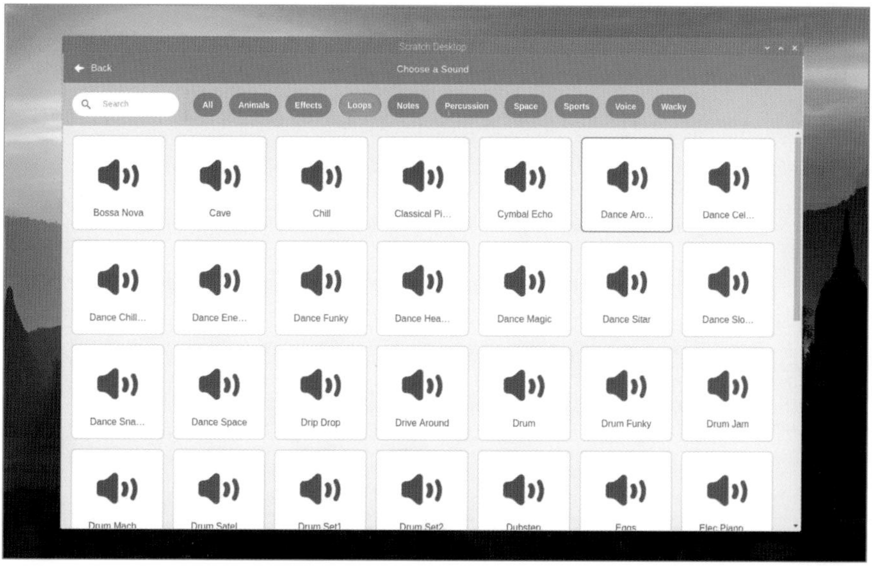

▲ **Figure 4-19:** Select a music loop from the sound library

Add another `when ⚑ clicked` Events block to your code area, then add a `forever` Control block. Inside this Control block, add a `play sound dance around until done` block – remembering to look for the name of whatever piece of music you chose – and click the green flag to test your new program. If you want to stop the music, click the red octagon to stop the program and silence the sound!

```
when  left arrow  ▼  key pressed
switch costume to  left ▼
turn ↺  15  degrees
```

```
when  right arrow  ▼  key pressed
switch costume to  right ▼
turn ↻  15  degrees
```

```
when  up arrow  ▼  key pressed
move  10  steps
```

```
when  down arrow  ▼  key pressed
move  -10  steps
```

```
when  ⚑ clicked
go to x:  0  y:  0
point in direction  90
repeat  6
    turn ↻  60  degrees
    create clone of  myself ▼
```

```
when  ⚑ clicked
forever
    play sound  Dance Around ▼  until done
```

Finally, you can simulate a full dancing routine by adding a new event trigger to your program. Add a `when space key pressed` Events block, then a `switch costume to right` block. Underneath this, add a `repeat 36` block – remembering to change the value from the default – and inside this a `turn ↻ 10 degrees` block and a `move 10 steps` block.

```
when  left arrow  ▼  key pressed
switch costume to  left ▼
turn ↺ 15 degrees
```

```
when  right arrow  ▼  key pressed
switch costume to  right ▼
turn ↻ 15 degrees
```

```
when  up arrow  ▼  key pressed
move 10 steps
```

```
when  down arrow  ▼  key pressed
move -10 steps
```

```
when 🚩 clicked
go to x: 0 y: 0
point in direction 90
repeat 6
  turn ↻ 60 degrees
  create clone of  myself ▼
```

```
when  space ▼  key pressed
switch costume to  right ▼
repeat 36
  turn ↻ 10 degrees
  move 10 steps
```

```
when 🚩 clicked
forever
  play sound  Dance Around ▼  until done
```

Click the green flag to start the program, then press the **SPACE** key to try out the new routine (**Figure 4-20**, overleaf)! Don't forget to save your program when you're finished.

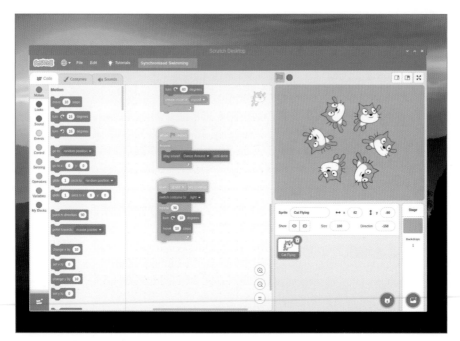

▲ **Figure 4-20:** The finished synchronised swimming routine

CHALLENGE: CUSTOM ROUTINE

Can you create your own synchronised swimming routine using loops? What would you need to change if you wanted more swimmers, or fewer swimmers? Can you add multiple swimming routines which can be triggered using different keys on the keyboard?

Project 3: **Archery Game**

Now you're getting to be a bit of an expert at Scratch, it's time to work on something a little more challenging: a game of archery, where the player has to hit a target with a randomly swaying bow and arrow.

ONLINE PROJECT

This project is also available online at **rpf.io/archery**

Start by opening the Chromium Web Browser and typing **rpf.io/p/en/archery-go** followed by the **ENTER** key. The resources for the game download as a zip file, so you'll need to unzip it (right-click it and select Extract Here). Switch back to Scratch 3 and click on the File menu followed by 'Load from your computer'. Click on **ArcheryResources.sb3** followed by the Open button. You'll be asked if you want to replace the contents of your current project: if you haven't saved your changes, click Cancel and save them, otherwise click OK.

▲ **Figure 4-21:** Resources project loaded for the archery game

The project you've just loaded contains a backdrop and a sprite (**Figure 4-21**), but none of the actual code to make a game: adding that in is your job. Start by adding a `when ⚑ clicked` block, then a `broadcast message1` block. Click on the down arrow at the end of the block and then 'New Message', and type in 'new arrow' before clicking the OK button. Your block now reads `broadcast new arrow`.

A broadcast is a message from one part of your program which can be received by any other part of your program. To have it actually do something, add a `when I receive message1` block, and again change it to read `when I receive new arrow`. This time you can just click on the down arrow and choose 'new arrow' from the list; you don't need to create the message again.

Below your `when I receive new arrow` block, add a `go to x: -150 y: -150` block and a `set size to 400 %` block. Remember that these aren't the default values for those blocks, so you'll need to change them once you've dragged them onto the code area. Click on the green flag to see what you've done so far: the arrow sprite, which the player uses to aim at the target, will jump to the bottom-left of the stage and quadruple in size.

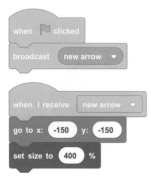

To give the player a challenge, add movement simulating swaying as the bow is drawn and the archer aims. Drag a `forever` block, followed by a `glide 1 seconds to x: -150 y: -150` block. Edit the first white box to say '0.5' instead of '1', then put a `pick random -150 to 150` Operators block in each of the other two white boxes. This means the arrow will drift around the stage in a random direction, for a random distance – making it far harder to hit the target!

```
when [flag] clicked
broadcast (new arrow ▼)

when I receive (new arrow ▼)
go to x: (-150) y: (-150)
set size to (400) %
forever
    glide (0.5) secs to x: (pick random (-150) to (150)) y: (pick random (-150) to (150))
```

Click the green flag again, and you'll see what that block does: your arrow sprite is now drifting around the stage, covering different parts of the target. At the moment, though, you have no way to loose the arrow at the target. Drag a `when space key pressed` block into your code area, followed by a `stop all` Control block. Click the down arrow at the end of the block and change it to a `stop other scripts in sprite` block.

```
when ▶ clicked
broadcast (new arrow ▼)

when I receive (new arrow ▼)
go to x: -150  y: -150
set size to 400 %
forever
    glide 0.5 secs to x: pick random -150 to 150 y: pick random -150 to 150

when space ▼ key pressed
stop other scripts in sprite ▼
```

If you'd stopped your program to add the new blocks, click the green flag to start it again and then press the **SPACE** key: you'll see the arrow sprite stop moving. That's a start, but you need to make it look like the arrow is flying to the target. Add a `repeat 50` block followed by a `change size by -10` block, then click the green flag to test your game again. This time, the arrow appears to be flying away from you and towards the target.

```
when ▶ clicked
broadcast (new arrow ▼)

when I receive (new arrow ▼)
go to x: -150  y: -150
set size to 400 %
forever
    glide 0.5 secs to x: pick random -150 to 150 y: pick random -150 to 150

when space ▼ key pressed
stop other scripts in sprite ▼
repeat 50
    change size by -10
```

To make the game fun, you need to add a way to keep score. Still in the same stack of blocks, add an `if then` block, making sure it's below the `repeat 50` block and not inside it, with a touching color? Sensing block in its diamond-shaped gap. To choose the correct colour, click on coloured box at the end of the Sensing block, then the eye-dropper icon 🖌, then click on the yellow bull's-eye of your target on the stage.

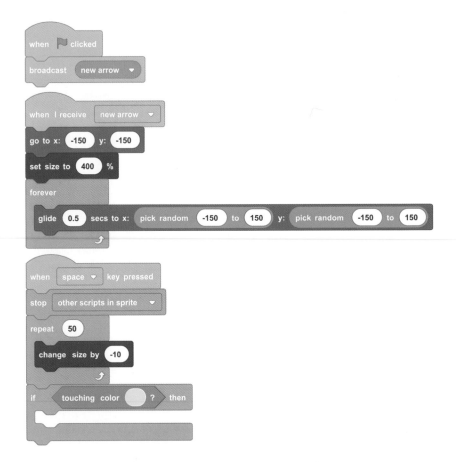

So that the player knows they have scored, add a start sound cheer block and a say 200 points for 2 seconds block inside the if then block. Finally, add a broadcast new arrow block to the very bottom of the block stack, below and outside the if then block, to give the player another arrow each time they fire one. Click the green flag to start your game, and try to hit the yellow bull's-eye: when you do, you'll be rewarded with a cheer from the crowd and a 200-point score!

```
when 🏳 clicked
broadcast  new arrow ▼
```

```
when I receive  new arrow ▼
go to x:  -150   y:  -150
set size to  400  %
forever
    glide  0.5  secs to x:  pick random  -150  to  150   y:  pick random  -150  to  150
```

```
when  space ▼  key pressed
stop  other scripts in sprite ▼
repeat  50
    change size by  -10
if  touching color    ?  then
    start sound  cheer ▼
    say  200 points  for  2  seconds
broadcast  new arrow ▼
```

For more Scratch projects to try, see **Appendix D: Further reading**

The game works, but is a little challenging. Using what you've learnt in this chapter, try extending it to add scores for hitting parts of the target other than the bull's-eye: 100 points for red, 50 points for blue, and so on.

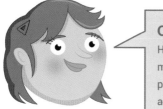

CHALLENGE: CAN YOU IMPROVE IT?
How would you make the game easier? How would you make it more difficult? Can you use variables to have the player's score increase as they fire more arrows? Can you add a countdown timer to put more pressure on the player?

Chapter 5

Programming with Python

Now you've got to grips with Scratch, we'll show you how to do text-based coding with Python

N amed after the Monty Python comedy troupe, Guido van Rossum's Python has grown from a hobby project first released to the public in 1991 to a much-loved programming language powering a wide range of projects. Unlike the visual environment of Scratch, Python is text based: you write instructions, using a simplified language and specific format, which the computer then carries out.

Python is a great next step for those who have already used Scratch, offering increased flexibility and a more 'traditional' programming environment. That's not to say it's difficult to learn, though: with a little practice, anyone can write Python programs for everything from simple calculations through to surprisingly complicated games.

This chapter builds on terms and concepts introduced in **Chapter 4, Programming with Scratch 3**. If you haven't worked through the exercises in that chapter yet, you'll find this chapter easier to follow if you go back and do so first.

Introducing the Thonny Python IDE

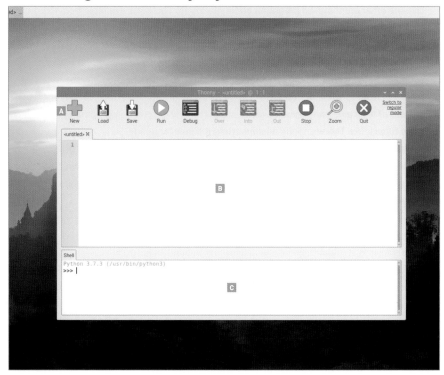

A **Toolbar** – Thonny's 'Simple Mode' interface uses a bar of friendly icons as its menu, allowing you to create, save, load, and run your Python programs, as well as test it in various ways.

B **Script Area** – The script area is where your Python programs are written, and is split into a main area for your program and a small side margin for showing line numbers.

C **Python Shell** – The Python shell allows you to type individual instructions which are then run as soon as you press the **ENTER** key, and also provides information about running programs.

THONNY VERSIONS ❗

Thonny has two interface versions: 'Normal Mode', and a 'Simple Mode' which is better for beginners. This chapter uses Simple Mode, which is loaded by default when you open Thonny from the Programming section of the raspberry menu.

Your first Python program: Hello, World!

Like the other pre-installed programs on Raspberry Pi, Thonny is available from the menu: click on the raspberry icon, move the cursor to the Programming section, and click on Thonny Python IDE. After a few seconds, the Thonny user interface (Simple Mode by default) will load.

Thonny is a package known as an *integrated development environment (IDE)*, a complicated-sounding name with a simple explanation: it gathers together, or *integrates*, all the different tools you need to write, or *develop*, software into a single user interface, or *environment*. There are lots of IDEs available, some of which support many different programming languages while others, like Thonny, focus on supporting a single language.

Unlike Scratch, which gives you visual building blocks as a basis for your program, Python is a more traditional programming language where everything is written down. Start your first program by clicking on the Python shell area at the bottom-left of the Thonny window, then type the following instruction before pressing the **ENTER** key:

```
print("Hello, World!")
```

When you press **ENTER**, you'll see that your program begins to run instantly: Python will respond, in the same shell area, with the message 'Hello, World!' (**Figure 5-1**), just as you asked. That's because the shell is a direct line to the Python *interpreter*, whose job it is to look at your instructions and *interpret* what they mean. This is known as *interactive mode*, and you can think of it like a face-to-face conversation with someone: as soon as you finish what you're saying, the other person will respond, then wait for whatever you say next.

▲ **Figure 5-1:** Python prints the 'Hello, World!' message in the shell area

SYNTAX ERROR

If your program doesn't run but instead prints a 'syntax error' message to the shell area, there's a mistake somewhere in what you've written. Python needs its instructions to be written in a very specific way: miss a bracket or a quotation mark, spell 'print' wrong or give it a capital P, or add extra symbols somewhere in the instruction and it won't run. Try typing the instruction again, and make sure it matches the version in this book before pressing the **ENTER** key!

You don't have to use Python in interactive mode, though. Click on the script area at the left-hand side of the Thonny window, then type your program again:

```
print("Hello, World!")
```

When you press the **ENTER** key this time, nothing happens — except that you get a new, blank line in the script area. To make this version of your program work, you'll have to click the Run icon ▶ in the Thonny toolbar. When you do, you'll be asked to save your program first; type a descriptive name, like 'Hello World' and click the Save button. Once your program has saved, you'll see two messages appear in the Python shell area (**Figure 5-2**):

```
>>> %Run 'Hello World.py'
    Hello, World!
```

▲ **Figure 5-2:** Running your simple program

The first of these lines is an instruction from Thonny telling the Python interpreter to run the program you just saved. The second is the output of the program – the message you told Python to print. Congratulations: you've now written and run your first Python program in both interactive and script modes!

CHALLENGE: NEW MESSAGE
?
Can you change the message the Python program prints as its output? If you wanted to add more messages, would you use interactive mode or script mode? What happens if you remove the brackets or the quotation marks from the program and then try to run it again?0.

Next steps: loops and code indentation

Just as Scratch uses stacks of jigsaw-like blocks to control which bits of the program are connected to which other bits, Python has its own way of controlling the sequence in which its programs run: *indentation*. Create a new program by clicking on the New icon ➕ in the Thonny toolbar. You won't lose your existing program; instead, Thonny will create a new tab above the script area. Start by typing in the following:

```python
print("Loop starting!")
for i in range (10):
```

The first line prints a simple message to the shell, just like your Hello World program. The second begins a *definite* loop, which works in the same way as in Scratch: a counter, **i**, is assigned to the loop and given a series of numbers – the **range** instruction, which is told to start at the number 0 and work upwards towards, but never reaching, the number 10 – to count. The colon symbol (**:**) tells Python that the next instruction should be part of the loop.

In Scratch, the instructions to be included in the loop are literally included inside the C-shaped block. Python uses a different approach: indenting code. The next line starts with four blank spaces, which Thonny should have added when you pressed **ENTER** after line 2:

```python
    print("Loop number", i)
```

The blank spaces push this line inwards compared to the other lines. This indentation is how Python tells the difference between instructions outside the loop and instructions inside the loop; the indented code is known as being nested.

You'll notice that when you pressed **ENTER** at the end of the third line, Thonny automatically indented the next line, assuming it would be part of the loop. To remove this, just press the **BACKSPACE** key once before typing the fourth line:

```
print("Loop finished!")
```

Your four-line program is now complete. The first line sits outside the loop, and will only run once; the second line sets up the loop; the third sits inside the loop and will run once for each time the loop loops; and the fourth line sits outside the loop once again.

```
print("Loop starting!")
for i in range (10):
    print("Loop number", i)
print("Loop finished!")
```

Click the Run icon, save the program as **Indentation**, and view the shell area for its output (**Figure 5-3**):

```
Loop starting!
Loop number 0
Loop number 1
Loop number 2
Loop number 3
Loop number 4
Loop number 5
Loop number 6
Loop number 7
Loop number 8
Loop number 9
Loop finished!
```

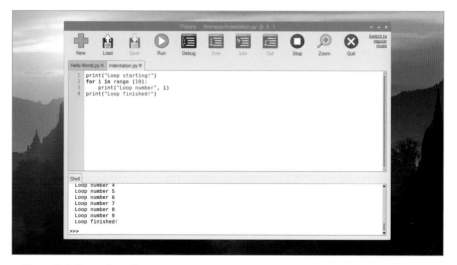

▲ **Figure 5-3:** Executing a loop

Indentation is a powerful part of Python, and one of the most common reasons for a program to not work as you expected. When looking for problems in a program, a process known as *debugging*, always double-check the indentation – especially when you begin nesting loops within loops.

Python also supports *infinite* loops, which run without end. To change your program from a definite loop to an infinite loop, edit line 2 to read:

```
while True:
```

If you click the Run icon now, you'll get an error: `name 'i' is not defined`. This is because you've deleted the line which created and assigned a value to the variable `i`. To fix this, simply edit line 3 so it no longer uses the variable:

```
print("Loop running!")
```

Click the Run icon, and – if you're quick – you'll see the 'Loop starting!' message followed by a never-ending string of 'Loop running' messages (**Figure 5-4**). The 'Loop finished!' message will never print, because the loop has no end: every time Python has finished printing the 'Loop running!' message, it goes back to the beginning of the loop and prints it again.

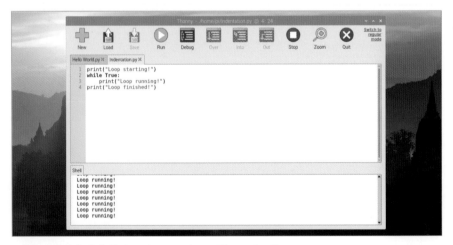

▲ **Figure 5-4:** An infinite loop keeps going until you stop the program

Click the Stop icon ⬤ on the Thonny toolbar to tell the program to stop what it's doing – known as interrupting the program. You'll see a message appear in the Python shell area, and the program will stop – and without ever reaching line 4.

CHALLENGE: LOOP THE LOOP

Can you change the loop back into a definite loop again? Can you add a second definite loop to the program? How would you add a loop within a loop, and how would you expect that to work?

Conditionals and variables

Variables, as in all programming languages, exist for more than just controlling loops. Start a new program by clicking the New icon ➕ on the Thonny menu, then type the following into the script area:

```
userName = input ("What is your name? ")
```

Click the Run icon, save your program as **Name Test**, and watch what happens in the shell area: you'll be asked for your name. Type your name into the shell area, followed by **ENTER**. Because that's the only instruction in your program, nothing else will happen (**Figure 5-5**). If you want to actually do anything with the data you've placed into the variable, you'll need more lines in your program.

▲ **Figure 5-5:** The input function lets you ask a user for some text input

To make your program do something useful with the name, add a *conditional statement* by typing the following:

```
if userName == "Clark Kent":
    print("You are Superman!")
else:
    print("You are not Superman!")
```

Remember that when Thonny sees that your code needs to be indented, it will do so automatically – but it doesn't know when your code needs to stop being indented, so you'll have to delete the spaces yourself.

Click the Run icon and enter your name into the shell area. Unless your name happens to be Clark Kent, you'll see the message 'You are not Superman!'. Click Run again, and this time type in the name 'Clark Kent' – making sure to write it exactly as in the program, with a capital C and K. This time, the program recognises that you are, in fact, Superman (**Figure 5-6**).

▲ **Figure 5-6:** Shouldn't you be out saving the world?

The == symbols tell Python to do a direct comparison, looking to see if the variable **userName** matches the text – known as a *string* – in your program. If you're working with numbers, there are other comparisons you can make: **>** to see if a number is greater than another number, **<** to see if it's less than, **=>** to see if it's equal to or greater than, **=<** to see if it's equal to or less than. There's also **!=**, which means not equal to – it's the exact opposite of ==. These symbols are technically known as *comparison operators*.

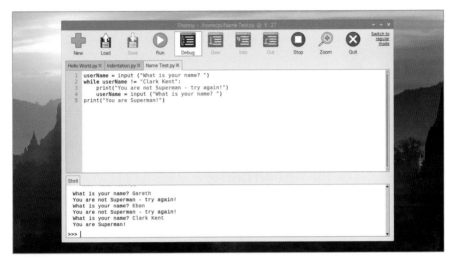

▲ **Figure 5-7:** It will keep asking for your name until you say it's 'Clark Kent'

USING = AND ==

The key to using variables is to learn the difference between = and ==. Remember: = means 'make this variable equal to this value', while == means 'check to see if the variable is equal to this value'. Mixing them up is a sure way to end up with a program that doesn't work!

Comparison operators can also be used in loops. Delete lines 2 through 5, then type the following in their place:

```python
while userName != "Clark Kent":
    print("You are not Superman - try again!")
    userName = input ("What is your name? ")
print("You are Superman!")
```

Click the Run icon again. This time, rather than quitting, the program will keep asking for your name until it confirms that you are Superman (**Figure 5-7**) – sort of like a very simple password. To get out of the loop, either type 'Clark Kent' or click the Stop icon on the Thonny toolbar. Congratulations: you now know how to use conditionals and comparison operators!

CHALLENGE: ADD MORE QUESTIONS ?

Can you change the program to ask more than one question, storing the answers in multiple variables? Can you make a program which uses conditionals and comparison operators to print whether a number typed in by the user is higher or lower than 5, like the program you created in **Chapter 4, Programming with Scratch**?

Project 1: **Turtle Snowflakes**

Now you understand how Python works, it's time to play with graphics and create a snowflake using a tool known as a *turtle*.

ONLINE PROJECT !

This project is also available online at **rpf.io/turtle-snowflakes**

Originally physical robots shaped like their animal namesakes, turtles are designed to move in a straight line, turn, and to lift and lower a pen – in the digital version, simply meaning to start or stop drawing a line as it moves. Unlike some other languages, namely Logo and its many variants, Python doesn't have a turtle tool built into it – but it comes with a *library* of add-on code to give it turtle power. Libraries are bundles of code which add new instructions to expand the capabilities of Python, and are brought into your own programs using an import command.

Create a new program by clicking on the New icon ✚, and type the following:

```
import turtle
```

When using instructions included in a library, you have to use the library name followed by a full stop, then the instruction name. That can be annoying to type out every time, so you can assign a shorter variable name instead – it could be just one letter, but we thought it might be nice for it to double as a pet name for the turtle. Type the following:

```
pat = turtle.Turtle()
```

To test your program out, you'll need to give your turtle something to do. Type:

```
pat.forward(100)
```

Click the Run icon, and save your program as **Turtle Snowflakes**. When the program has saved, a new window called 'Turtle Graphics' will appear and you'll see the result of your program: your turtle, Pat, will move forwards 100 units, drawing a straight line (**Figure 5-8**).

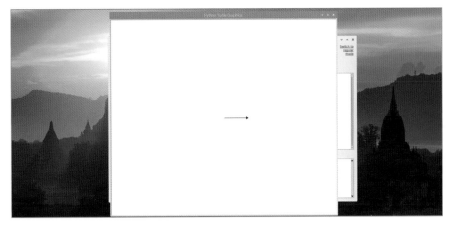

▲ **Figure 5-8:** The turtle moves forward to draw a straight line

Switch back to the main Thonny window – if it's hidden behind the Turtle Graphics window, either click the minimize button on the Turtle Graphics window or click on the Thonny entry in the task bar at the top of the screen – and click the Stop button to close the Turtle Graphics window.

Typing out every single movement instruction by hand would be tedious, so delete line 3 and create a loop to do the hard work of creating shapes:

```
for i in range(2):
    pat.forward(100)
    pat.right(60)
    pat.forward(100)
    pat.right(120)
```

Run your program, and Pat will draw a single parallelogram (**Figure 5-9**).

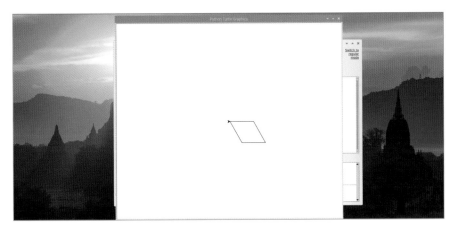

▲ **Figure 5-9:** By combining turns and movements, you can draw shapes

To turn that into a snowflake-like shape, click the Stop icon in the main Thonny window and create a loop around your loop by adding the following line as line 3:

```
for i in range(10):
```

...and the following at the bottom of your program:

```
    pat.right(36)
```

Your program won't run as it is, because the existing loop isn't indented correctly. To fix that, click on the start of each line in the existing loop – lines 4 through 8 – and press the **SPACE** key four times to correct the indentation. Your program should now look like this:

```
import turtle
pat = turtle.Turtle()
for i in range(10):
    for i in range(2):
        pat.forward(100)
        pat.right(60)
        pat.forward(100)
        pat.right(120)
    pat.right(36)
```

Click the Run icon, and watch the turtle: it'll draw a parallelogram, as before, but when it's done it'll turn 36 degrees and draw another, then another, and so on until there are ten overlapping parallelograms on the screen – looking a little like a snowflake (**Figure 5-10**).

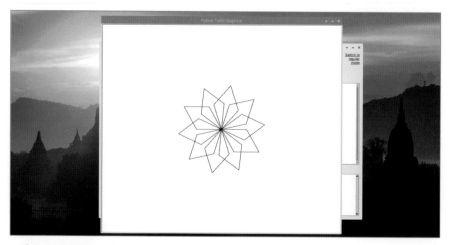

▲ **Figure 5-10:** Repeating the shape to make a more complex one

While a robotic turtle draws in a single colour on a large piece of paper, Python's simulated turtle can use a range of colours. Add a new line 3 and 4, pushing the existing lines down:

```
turtle.Screen().bgcolor("blue")
pat.color("cyan")
```

Run your program again and you'll see the effect of your new code: the background colour of the Turtle Graphics window has changed to blue, and the snowflake is now cyan (**Figure 5-11**).

▲ **Figure 5-11:** Changing the background and snowflake colours

You can also have the colours chosen randomly from a list, using the **random** library. Go back to the top of your program and insert the following as line 2:

```
import random
```

Change the background colour in what is now line 4 from 'blue' to 'grey', then create a new variable called 'colours' by inserting a new line 5:

```
colours = ["cyan", "purple", "white", "blue"]
```

U.S. SPELLINGS

Many programming languages use American English spellings, and Python is no exception: the command for changing the colour of the turtle's pen is spelled *color*, and if you spell it the British English way as *colour* it simply won't work. Variables, though, can have any spelling you like – which is why you're able to call your new variable *colours* and have Python understand.

This type of variable is known as a list, and is marked by square brackets. In this case, the list is filled with possible colours for the snowflake segments – but you still need to tell Python to choose one each time the loop repeats. At the very end of the program, enter the following – making sure it's indented with four spaces so it forms part of the outer loop, just like the line above it:

```
pat.color(random.choice(colours))
```

Click the Run icon and the snowflake-stroke-ninja-star will be drawn again. This time, though, Python will choose a random colour from your list as it draws each petal – giving the snowflake a pleasing, multicolour finish (**Figure 5-12**).

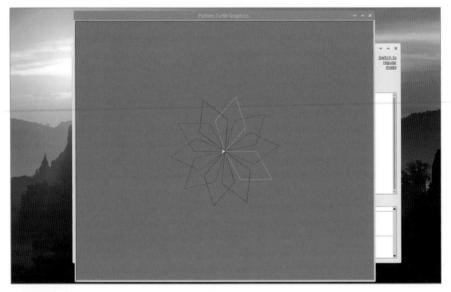

▲ **Figure 5-12:** Using random colours for the 'petals'

To make the snowflake look less like a ninja star and more like an actual snowflake, add a new line 6, directly below your **colours** list, and type the following:

```
pat.penup()
pat.forward(90)
pat.left(45)
pat.pendown()
```

The **penup** and **pendown** instructions would move a physical pen off and on to the paper if using a turtle robot, but in the virtual world simply tell your turtle to stop and start drawing lines. This time though, rather than using a loop, you're going to be creating a *function* – a segment of code which you can call at any time, like creating your very own Python instruction.

Start by deleting the code for drawing your parallelogram-based snowflakes: that's everything between and including the **pat.color("cyan")** instruction on line 10 through to **pat.right(36)** on line 17. Leave the **pat.color(random.choice(colours))** instruction, but add a hash symbol (#) at the start of the line. This is known as *commenting out* an instruction, and means that Python will ignore it. You can use comments to add explanations to your code, which will make it a lot easier to understand when you come back to it a few months later or send it on to someone else!

Create your function, which will be called 'branch', by typing the following instruction onto line 10, below **pat.pendown():**

```
def branch():
```

This *defines* your function, **branch**. When you press the **ENTER** key, Thonny will automatically add indentation for the function's instructions. Type the following, making sure to pay close attention to indentation – because at one point you're going to be nesting code three indentation levels deep!

```
for i in range(3):
    for i in range(3):
        pat.forward(30)
        pat.backward(30)
        pat.right(45)
    pat.left(90)
    pat.backward(30)
    pat.left(45)
pat.right(90)
pat.forward(90)
```

Finally, create a new loop at the bottom of your program – but above the commented-out colour line – to run, or *call*, your new function:

```
for i in range(8):
    branch()
    pat.left(45)
```

Your finished program should look like this:

```python
import turtle
import random
pat = turtle.Turtle()
turtle.Screen().bgcolor("grey")
colours = ["cyan", "purple", "white", "blue"]
pat.penup()
pat.forward(90)
pat.left(45)
pat.pendown()
def branch():
    for i in range(3):
        for i in range(3):
            pat.forward(30)
            pat.backward(30)
            pat.right(45)
        pat.left(90)
        pat.backward(30)
        pat.left(45)
    pat.right(90)
    pat.forward(90)
for i in range(8):
    branch()
    pat.left(45)
#    pat.color(random.choice(colours))
```

Click on Run and watch the graphics window as Pat draws by following your instructions. Congratulations: your snowflake now looks a lot more like a snowflake (**Figure 5-13**)!

▲ **Figure 5-13:** Extra branches make it look like a snowflake

CHALLENGE: WHAT NEXT?

Can you use your commented-out instruction to have the branches of the snowflake drawn in different colours? Can you create a 'snowflake' function, and use it to draw lots of snowflakes on the screen? Can you have your program change the size and colour of the snowflakes at random?

Project 2: **Scary Spot the Difference**

Python can also handle pictures and sounds as well as turtle-based graphics, which can be used to great effect as a prank on your friends — a spot-the-difference game with a scary secret at its heart, perfect for Halloween!

ONLINE PROJECT

This project is also available online at **rpf.io/scary-spot**

This project needs two images — your spot-the-difference image plus a 'scary' surprise image — and a sound file. Click on the raspberry icon to load the Raspbian menu, choose the Internet category, and click on Chromium Web Browser. When it has loaded, type **rpf.io/spot-pic** into the address bar followed by the **ENTER** key. Right-click on the picture and click on 'Save image as...', choose the Home folder from the list on the left-hand side, then click Save. Click back on Chromium's address bar, then type **rpf.io/scary-pic** followed by the **ENTER** key. As before, right-click the picture, click 'Save image as...', choose the Home folder, then click Save.

For the sound file you'll need, click back into the address bar and type **rpf.io/scream** followed by the **ENTER** key. This file, the sound of a scream to give your player a real surprise, will play automatically — but it will need to be saved before you can use it. Right-click on the small audio player, click 'Save as...', choose the Home folder, and click Save. You can now close the Chromium window.

Click the New icon in the Thonny toolbar to begin a new project. As before, you're going to be using a library to extend Python's capabilities: the Pygame library, which as the name suggests was created with games in mind. Type the following:

```
import pygame
```

You'll need some parts of other libraries, and from a subsection of the Pygame library, too. Import these by typing the following:

```
from pygame.locals import *
from time import sleep
from random import randrange
```

The **from** instruction works differently to the **import** instruction, allowing you to import only the parts of a library you need rather than the whole library. Next, you need to set up Pygame; this is known as *initialisation*. Pygame needs to know the width and height of the player's monitor or TV, known as its *resolution*. Type the following:

```
pygame.init()
width = pygame.display.Info().current_w
height = pygame.display.Info().current_h
```

The final step in setting Pygame up is to create its window, which Pygame calls a screen. Type the following:

```
screen = pygame.display.set_mode((width, height))

pygame.quit()
```

Note the blank line in the middle; this is where your program will go. For now, though, click on the Run icon, save your program as **Spot the Difference**, and watch: Pygame will create a window, filling it with a black background, which will then almost immediately disappear as it reaches the instruction to quit. Aside from a short message in the shell (**Figure 5-14**), the program hasn't achieved much so far.

▲ **Figure 5-14:** Your program is functional, but doesn't do much yet

To display your spot-the-difference image, type in the following line in the space above `pygame.quit()`:

```
difference = pygame.image.load('spot_the_diff.png')
```

To make sure the image fills the screen, you'll need to scale it to match your monitor or TV's resolution. Type the following:

```
difference = pygame.transform.scale(difference, (width, height))
```

Now the image is in memory, you need to tell Pygame to actually display it on the screen – a process known as *blitting*, or a *bit block transfer*. Type the following:

```
screen.blit(difference, (0, 0))
pygame.display.update()
```

The first of these lines copies the image onto the screen, starting at the top-left corner; the second tells Pygame to redraw the screen. Without this second line, the image will be in the correct place in memory but you'll never see it!

Click the Run icon, and the image will briefly appear on screen (**Figure 5-15**).

▲ **Figure 5-15:** Your spot-the-difference image

To see the image for longer, add the following line just above **pygame.quit()**:

```
sleep(3)
```

Click Run again, and the image will stay on the screen for longer. Add your surprise image by typing the following just below the line **pygame.display.update()**:

```
zombie = pygame.image.load('scary_face.png')
zombie = pygame.transform.scale(zombie, (width, height))
```

Add a delay, so the zombie image doesn't appear right away:

```
sleep(3)
```

Then blit the image to the screen and update so it shows to the player:

```
screen.blit(zombie, (0,0))
pygame.display.update()
```

Click the Run icon and watch what happens: Pygame will load your spot-the-difference image, but after three seconds it will be replaced with the scary zombie (**Figure 5-16**)!

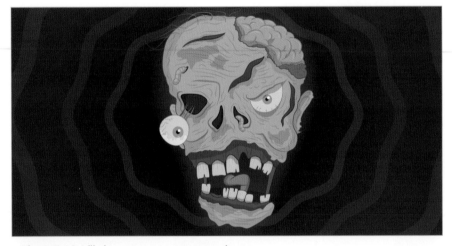

▲ **Figure 5-16:** It'll give someone a scary surprise

Having the delay set at three seconds, though, makes things a bit predictable. Change the line **sleep(3)** above **screen.blit(zombie, (0,0))** to:

```
sleep(randrange(5, 15))
```

This picks a random number between 5 and 15 and delays the program for that long. Next, add the following line just above your **sleep** instruction to load the scream sound file:

```
scream = pygame.mixer.Sound('scream.wav')
```

Move below your **sleep** instruction and type the following on a new line to start the sound playing, so it kicks in just ahead of the scary image actually being shown to the player.

```
scream.play()
```

Finally, tell Pygame to stop playing the sound by typing the following line just above `pygame.quit()`:

```
scream.stop()
```

Click the Run icon and admire your handiwork: after a few seconds of innocent spot-the-difference fun, your scary zombie will appear alongside a blood-curdling shriek – sure to give your friends a fright! If you find that the zombie picture appears before the sound starts playing, you can compensate by adding a small delay just after your `scream.play()` instruction and before your `screen.blit` instruction:

```
sleep(0.4)
```

Your finished program should look like this:

```
import pygame
from pygame.locals import *
from time import sleep
from random import randrange
pygame.init()
width = pygame.display.Info().current_w
height = pygame.display.Info().current_h
screen = pygame.display.set_mode((width, height))
difference = pygame.image.load('spot_the_diff.png')
difference = pygame.transform.scale(difference, (width, height))
screen.blit(difference, (0, 0))
pygame.display.update()
zombie = pygame.image.load('scary_face.png')
zombie = pygame.transform.scale (zombie, (width, height))
scream = pygame.mixer.Sound('scream.wav')
sleep(randrange(5, 15))
scream.play()
screen.blit(zombie, (0,0))
pygame.display.update()
sleep(3)
scream.stop()
pygame.quit()
```

Now all that's left to do is to invite your friends to play spot-the-difference – and to make sure the speakers are turned up, of course!

CHALLENGE: ALTER THE LOOK

Can you change the images to make the prank more appropriate for other events, like Christmas? Can you draw your own spot-the-difference and scary images (using a graphics editor such as GIMP)? Could you track the user clicking on a difference, to make it more convincing?

Project 3: **RPG Maze**

Now you're getting the hang of Python, it's time to use Pygame to make something a little more complicated: a fully-functional text-based maze game, based on classic role-playing games. Known as text adventures or interactive fiction, these games date back to when computers couldn't handle graphics but still have their fans who argue that no graphics will ever be as vivid as those you have in your imagination!

ONLINE PROJECT

This project is also available online at **rpf.io/python-rpg**

This program is quite a bit more complex than the others in this chapter, so to make things easier you will start with a version already partially written. Open the Chromium Web Browser and go to the following address: **rpf.io/rpg-code**.

The Chromium Web Browser will automatically download the code for the program to your Downloads folder, but will warn you that the type of file – a Python program – could harm your computer. You've downloaded the file from the Raspberry Pi Foundation, a trusted source, so click on the Keep button of the warning message that appears at the bottom of the screen.Go back to Thonny, then click the Load icon 📁. Find the file, **rpg-rpg.py**, in your Downloads folder and click the Load button.;

Start by clicking the Run icon to familiarise yourself with how a text adventure works. The game's output appears in the shell area at the bottom of the Thonny window; make the Thonny window larger by clicking on the maximise button to make it easier to read.

The game, as it stands now, is very simple: there are two rooms and no objects. The player starts in the Hall, the first of the two rooms. To go to the Kitchen, simply type 'go south' followed by the **ENTER** key (**Figure 5-17**). When you're in the Kitchen, you can type 'go north' to return to the Hall. You can also try typing 'go west' and 'go east', but as there aren't any rooms in those directions the game will show you an error message.

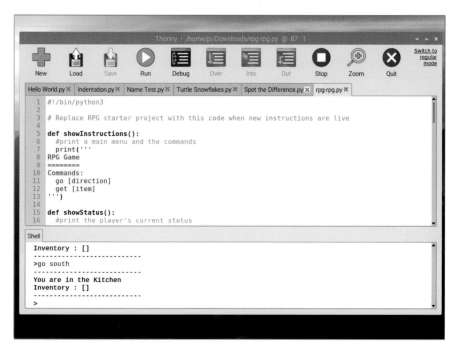

▲ **Figure 5-17:** There are only two rooms so far

Scroll down to line 29 of the program in the script area to find a variable called **rooms**. This type of variable is known as a *dictionary*, and tells the game the rooms, their exits, and which room a given exit leads to.

To make the game more interesting, add another room: a Dining Room, east of the Hall. Find the **rooms** variable in the scripts area, and extend it by adding a comma symbol (**,**) after the **}** on line 38 then typing the following (exact indentation isn't essential in a dictionary):

```
'Dining Room' : {
       'west' : 'Hall'
    }
```

You'll also need a new exit in the Hall, as one isn't automatically created for you. Go to the end of line 33, add a comma, then add the following line:

```
'east' : 'Dining Room'
```

Click the Run icon, and try your new room: type 'go east' while in the Hall to enter the Dining Room (**Figure 5-18**, overleaf), and type 'go west' while in the Dining Room to enter the Hall. Congratulations: you've made a room of your own!

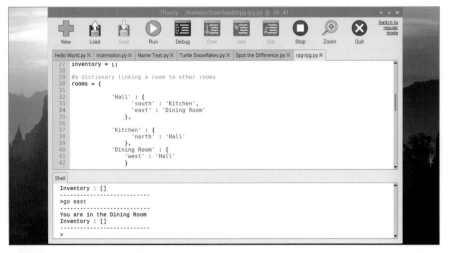

▲ **Figure 5-18:** You have added another room

Empty rooms aren't much fun, though. To add an item to a room, you'll need to modify that room's dictionary. Stop the program by clicking the Stop icon. Find the **Hall** dictionary in the scripts area, then add a comma to the end of the line **'east' : 'Dining Room'** before pressing **ENTER** and typing the following line:

```
'item' : 'key'
```

Click on Run again. This time, the game will tell you that you can see your new item: a key. Type 'get key' (**Figure 5-19**) and you can pick it up, adding it to the list of items you're carrying – known as your *inventory*. Your inventory stays with you as you travel from room to room.

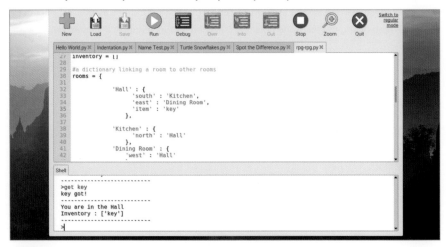

▲ **Figure 5-19:** The collected key is added to your inventory

Click the Stop icon ⬤, and make the game more interesting by adding a monster to avoid. Find the **Kitchen** dictionary, and add a 'monster' item in the same way as you added the 'key' item – remembering to add a comma to the end of the line above:

```
'item' : 'monster'
```

To have the monster be able to attack the player, you'll need to add some logic to the game. Scroll to the very bottom of the program in the script area and add the following lines – including the comment, marked with a hash symbol, which will help you understand the program if you come back to it another day – and make sure to indent the lines:

```
# player loses if they enter a room with a monster
if 'item' in rooms[currentRoom] and 'monster' in
rooms[currentRoom]['item']:
        print('A monster has got you... GAME OVER!')
        break
```

Click Run, and try going into the Kitchen room (**Figure 5-20**) – the monster won't be too impressed when you do!

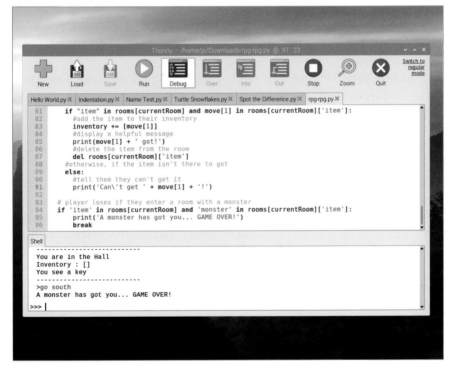

▲ **Figure 5-20:** Never mind rats, there's a monster in the kitchen

To turn this adventure into a proper game, you're going to need more items, another room, and the ability to 'win' by leaving the house with all the items safely in your inventory. Start by adding another room, just as you did for the Dining Room – only this time, it's a Garden. Add an exit from the Dining Room dictionary, remembering to add a comma to the end of the line above:

```
'south' : 'Garden'
```

Then add your new room to the main **rooms** dictionary, again remembering to add a comma after the } on the line above as before:

```
'Garden' : {
        'north' : 'Dining Room'
    }
```

Add a 'potion' object to the Dining Room dictionary, again remembering to add the necessary comma to the line above:

```
'item' : 'potion'
```

Finally, scroll to the bottom of the program and add the logic required to check if the player has all the items and, if so, tell them they've won the game:

```
# player wins if they get to the garden with a key and a potion
    if currentRoom == 'Garden' and 'key' in inventory and
'potion' in inventory:
        print('You escaped the house... YOU WIN!')
        break
```

Click Run, and try to finish the game by picking up the key and the potion before going to the garden. Remember not to enter the Kitchen room, because that's where the monster is!

As a last tweak for the game, add some instructions telling the player how to complete the game. Scroll to the top of the program, where the function **showInstructions()** is defined, and add the following:

```
Get to the Garden with a key and a potion
Avoid the monsters!
```

Run the game one last time, and you'll see your new instructions appear at the very start (**Figure 5-21**). Congratulations: you've made an interactive text-based maze game!

▲ **Figure 5-21:** Now the player knows what they need to do

CHALLENGE: EXPAND THE GAME

Can you add more rooms to make the game last longer?
Can you add an item to protect you from the monster?
How would you add a weapon to slay the monster? Can
you add rooms that are above and below the existing
rooms, accessed by stairs?

Chapter 6

Physical computing with Scratch and Python

There's more to coding than doing things on screen – you can also control electronic components connected to your Raspberry Pi's GPIO pins

When people think of 'programming' or 'coding', they're usually – and naturally – thinking about software. Coding can be about more than just software, though: it can affect the real world through hardware. This is known as *physical computing*. As the name suggests, physical computing is all about controlling things in the real world with your programs: hardware, rather than software. When you set the program on your washing machine, change the temperature on your programmable thermostat, or press a button at traffic lights to cross the road safely, you're using physical computing.

Raspberry Pi is a great device for learning about physical computing thanks to one key feature: the *general-purpose input/output* (*GPIO*) header.

Introducing the GPIO header

Found at the top edge of Raspberry Pi's circuit board and looking like two long rows of metal pins, the GPIO header is how you can connect hardware like light-emitting diodes (LEDs) and switches to Raspberry Pi for control under programs you create. The name might sound a little confusing, but it describes the component well: its pins can be used for both input and output, they have no fixed purpose, and when rows of pins are exposed on a circuit board like this they're known as a header. Thus: 'general-purpose input/output header'.

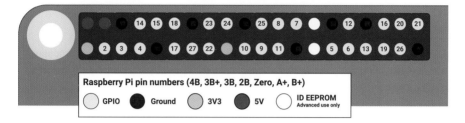

Raspberry Pi's GPIO header is made up of 40 male pins. Some pins are available for you to use in your physical computing projects, some pins provide power, while other pins are reserved for communicating with add-on hardware like the Sense HAT (see **Chapter 7**).

There are several categories of pin types, each of which has a particular function:

3V3	**3.3 volts power**	A permanently-on source of 3.3 V power, the same voltage Raspberry Pi runs at internally
5V	**5 volts power**	A permanently-on source of 5 V power, the same voltage as Raspberry Pi takes in at the micro USB power connector
Ground (GND)	**0 volts ground**	A ground connection, used to complete a circuit connected to power source
GPIO XX	**General-purpose input/output pin number 'XX'**	The GPIO pins available for your programs, identified by a number from 2 to 27
ID EEPROM	**Reserved special-purpose pins**	Pins reserved for use with Hardware Attached on Top (HAT) and other accessories

Electronic components

The GPIO header is only part of what you'll need to begin working with physical computing;
the other half is made up of electrical components, the devices you'll control from the GPIO
header. There are thousands of different components available, but most GPIO projects are
made using the following common parts.

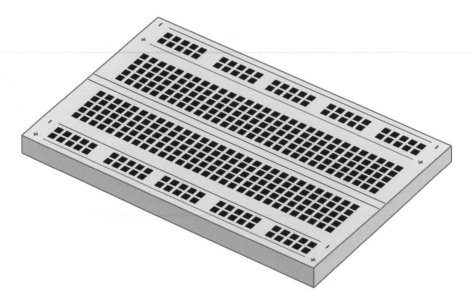

A *breadboard*, also known as a *solderless breadboard*, can make physical computing projects
considerably easier. Rather than having a bunch of separate components which need to be
connected with wires, a breadboard lets you insert components and have them connected
through metal tracks which are hidden beneath its surface. Many breadboards also include
sections for power distribution, making it easier to build your circuits. You don't need a
breadboard to get started with physical computing, but it certainly helps.

Jumper wires, also known as *jumper leads*, connect
components to your Raspberry Pi and, if you're not using
a breadboard, to each other. They are available in three
versions: male-to-female (M2F), which you'll need to connect
a breadboard to the GPIO pins; female-to-female (F2F), which
can be used to connect individual components together if
you're not using a breadboard; and male-to-male (M2M), which
is used to make connections from one part of a breadboard
to another. Depending on your project, you may need all three
types of jumper wire; if you're using a breadboard, you can
usually get away with just M2F and M2M jumper wires.

A *push-button switch*, also known as a *momentary
switch*, is the type of switch you'd use to control a games
console. Commonly available with two or four legs – either
type will work with Raspberry Pi – the push-button is an
input device: you can tell your program to watch out for it
being pushed and then perform a task. Another common
switch type is a *latching switch*; whereas a push-button is
only active while you're holding it down, a latching switch –
like you'd find in a light switch – activates when you toggle
it once, then stays active until you toggle it again.

A *light-emitting diode* (*LED*) is an *output device*; you control it directly
from your program. An LED lights up when it's on, and you'll find them
all over your house, ranging from the small ones which let you know
when you've left your washing machine switched on, to the large ones
you might have lighting up your rooms. LEDs are available in a wide
range of shapes, colours, and sizes, but not all are suitable for use with
Raspberry Pi: avoid any which say they are designed for 5 V or 12 V
power supplies.

Resistors are components which control the flow of *electrical
current*, and are available in different values measured using a
unit called *ohms* (Ω). The higher the number of ohms, the more
resistance is provided. For Raspberry Pi physical computing
projects, their most common use is to protect LEDs from drawing
too much current and damaging themselves or your Raspberry
Pi; for this you'll want resistors rated at around 330 Ω, though
many electrical suppliers sell handy packs containing a number of
different commonly used values to give you more flexibility.

A *piezoelectric buzzer*, usually just called a buzzer or a sounder, is another output device. Whereas an LED produces light, though, a buzzer produces a noise – a buzzing noise, in fact. Inside the buzzer's plastic housing are a pair of metal plates; when active, these plates vibrate against each other to produce the buzzing sound. There are two types of buzzer: *active buzzers* and *passive buzzers*. Make sure to get an active buzzer, as these are the simplest to use.

Other common electrical components include motors, which need a special control board before they can be connected to Raspberry Pi, infrared sensors which detect movement, temperature and humidity sensors which can be used to predict the weather, and light-dependent resistors (LDRs) – input devices which operate like a reverse LED by detecting light.

Sellers all over the world provide components for physical computing with Raspberry Pi, either as individual parts or in kits which provide everything you need to get started. Some of the most popular retailers are:

- **RS Components** – uk.rs-online.com
- **CPC** – cpc.farnell.com
- **Pimoroni** – pimoroni.com
- **Pi Hut** – thepihut.com
- **ModMyPi** – modmypi.com
- **PiSupply** – uk.pi-supply.com
- **Adafruit** – adafruit.com

To complete the projects in this chapter, you should have at least:

- 3 × LEDs: red, green, and yellow or amber
- 3 × 330 Ω resistors
- 2 × push-button switches
- 1 × active buzzer
- Male-to-female (M2F) and female-to-female (F2F) jumper wires
- Optionally, a breadboard and male-to-male (M2M) jumper wires

Reading resistor colour codes

Resistors come in a wide range of values, from zero-resistance versions which are effectively just pieces of wire to high-resistance versions the size of your leg. Very few of these resistors have their values printed on them in numbers, though: instead, they use a special code printed as coloured stripes or bands around the body of the resistor.

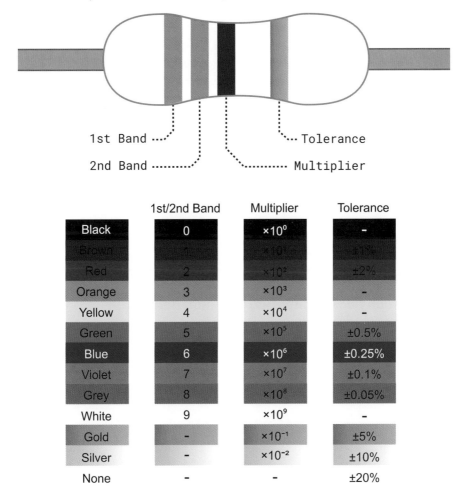

	1st/2nd Band	Multiplier	Tolerance
Black	0	$\times 10^0$	-
Brown	1	$\times 10^1$	±1%
Red	2	$\times 10^2$	±2%
Orange	3	$\times 10^3$	-
Yellow	4	$\times 10^4$	-
Green	5	$\times 10^5$	±0.5%
Blue	6	$\times 10^6$	±0.25%
Violet	7	$\times 10^7$	±0.1%
Grey	8	$\times 10^8$	±0.05%
White	9	$\times 10^9$	-
Gold	-	$\times 10^{-1}$	±5%
Silver	-	$\times 10^{-2}$	±10%
None	-	-	±20%

To read the value of a resistor, position it so the group of bands is to the left and the lone band is to the right. Starting from the first band, look its colour up in the '1st/2nd Band' column of the table to get the first and second digits. This example has two orange bands, which both mean a value of '3' for a total of '33'. If your resistor has four grouped bands instead of three, note down the value of the third band too (for five/six-band resistors, see **rpf.io/5-6band**).

Moving onto the last grouped band – the third or fourth – look its colour up in the 'Multiplier' column. This tells you what number you need to multiply your current number by to get the actual value of the resistor. This example has a brown band, which means '×10¹'. That may look confusing, but it's simply *scientific notation*: '×10¹' simply means 'add one zero to the end of your number'. If it were blue, for ×10⁶, it would mean 'add six zeroes to the end of your number'.

33, from the orange bands, plus the added zero from the brown band gives us 330 – which is the value of the resistor, measured in ohms. The final band, on the right, is the *tolerance* of the resistor. This is simply how close to its rated value it is likely to be. Cheaper resistors might have a silver band, indicating it can be 10 percent higher or lower than its rating, or no last band at all, indicating it can be 20 percent higher or lower; the most expensive resistors have a grey band, indicating that it will be within 0.05 percent of its rating. For hobbyist projects, accuracy isn't that important: any tolerance will usually work fine.

If your resistor value goes above 1000 ohms (1000 Ω), it is usually rated in kilohms (kΩ); if it goes above a million ohms, those are megohms (MΩ). A 2200 Ω resistor would be written as 2.2 kΩ; a 2200000 Ω resistor would be written as 2.2 MΩ.

CAN YOU WORK IT OUT?

What colour bands would a 100 Ω resistor have? What colour bands would a 2.2 MΩ resistor have? If you wanted to find the cheapest resistors, what colour tolerance band would you look for?

Your first physical computing program: Hello, LED!

Just as printing 'Hello, World' to the screen is a fantastic first step in learning a programming language, making an LED light up is the traditional introduction to learning physical computing. For this project, you'll need an LED and a 330 ohm (330 Ω) resistor, or as close to 330 Ω as you can find, plus female-to-female (F2F) jumper wires.

RESISTANCE IS VITAL

The resistor is a vital component in this circuit: it protects Raspberry Pi and the LED by limiting the amount of electrical current the LED can draw. Without it, the LED can pull too much current and burn itself – or Raspberry Pi – out. When used like this, the resistor is known as a *current-limiting resistor*. The exact value of resistor you need depends on the LED you're using, but 330 Ω works for most common LEDs. The higher the value, the dimmer the LED; the lower the value, the brighter the LED.

Never connect an LED to a Raspberry Pi without a current-limiting resistor, unless you know the LED has a built-in resistor of appropriate value.

Start by checking that your LED works. Turn your Raspberry Pi so the GPIO header is in two vertical strips to the right-hand side. Connect one end of your 330 Ω resistor to the first 3.3 V pin (labelled 3V3 in **Figure 6-1**) using a female-to-female jumper wire, then connect the other end to the long leg – positive, or anode – of your LED with another female-to-female jumper wire. Take a last female-to-female jumper wire, and connect the short leg – negative, or cathode – of your LED to the first ground pin (labelled GND in **Figure 6-1**).

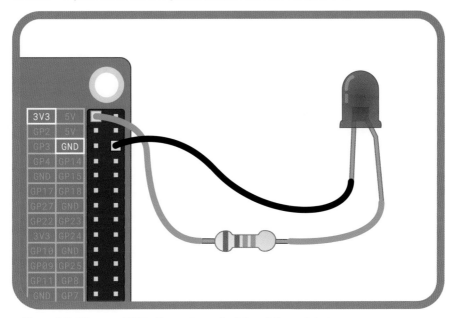

▲ **Figure 6-1:** Wire your LED to these pins – don't forget the resistor!

As long as your Raspberry Pi is on, the LED should light up. If it doesn't, double-check your circuit: make sure you haven't used too high a resistor value, that all the wires are properly connected, and that you've definitely picked the right GPIO pins to match the diagram. Also check the legs of the LED, as LEDs will only work one way around: with the longer leg connected to the positive side of the circuit and the shorter leg to the negative.

Once your LED is working, it's time to program it. Disconnect the jumper wire from the 3.3 V pin (labelled 3V3 in **Figure 6-2**, overleaf) and connect it to the GPIO 25 pin (labelled GP25 in **Figure 6-2**). The LED will switch off, but don't worry – that's normal.

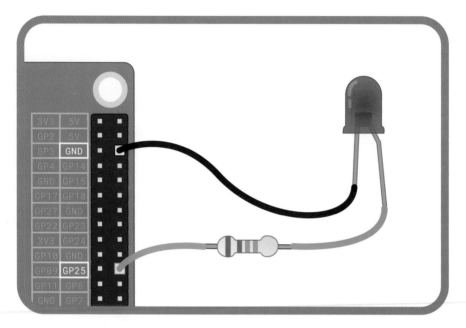

▲ **Figure 6-2:** Disconnect the wire from 3V3 and connect it to the GPIO 25 pin

You are now ready to create a Scratch or Python program to turn your LED on and off.

CODING KNOWLEDGE

The projects in this chapter need you to be comfortable with using Scratch 3 and the Thonny Python integrated development environment (IDE). If you haven't already done so, turn to **Chapter 4, Programming with Scratch 3**, and **Chapter 5, Programming with Python**, and work through those projects first.

LED control in Scratch

Load Scratch 3 and click on the Add Extension icon 🖾. Scroll down to find the 'Raspberry Pi GPIO' extension (**Figure 6-3**), then click on it.. This loads the blocks you need to control Raspberry Pi's GPIO header from Scratch 3. You'll see the new blocks appear in the blocks palette; when you need them, they're available in the Raspberry Pi GPIO category.

▲ **Figure 6-3:** Add the Raspberry Pi GPIO extension to Scratch 3

Start by dragging a `when ▶ clicked` Events block onto the code area, then place a `set gpio to output high` block underneath it. You'll need to choose the number of the pin you're using: click on the small arrow to open the drop-down selection and click on '25' to tell Scratch you're controlling the GPIO 25 pin.

Click the green flag to run your program. You'll see your LED light up: you've programmed your first physical computing project! Click the red octagon to stop your program: notice how the LED stays lit? That's because your program only ever told Raspberry Pi to turn the LED on – that's what the 'output high' part of your `set gpio 25 to output high` block means. To turn it off again, click on the down arrow at the end of the block and choose 'low' from the list.

Click the green flag again, and this time your program turns the LED off. To make things more interesting, add a `forever` control block and a couple of `wait 1 seconds` blocks to create a program to flash the LED on and off every second.

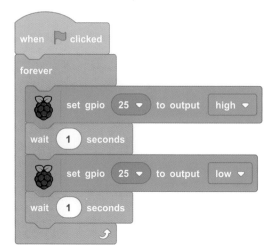

Click the green flag and watch your LED: it will turn on for a second, turn off for a second, turn on for a second, and keep repeating that pattern until you click the red octagon to stop it. See what happens when you click the octagon while the LED is in its on or off states.

CHALLENGE: CAN YOU ALTER IT?

How would you change the program to make the LED stay on for longer? What about staying off for longer? What's the smallest delay you can use while still seeing the LED switch on and off?

LED control in Python

Load Thonny from the Programming section of the raspberry menu, then click the New button to start a new project and Save to save it as **Hello LED**. To use the GPIO pins from Python, you need a library called GPIO Zero. For this project, you only need the part of the library for working with LEDs. Import just this section of the library by typing the following into the Python shell area:

```
from gpiozero import LED
```

Next, you need to let GPIO Zero know which GPIO pin the LED is connected to. Type the following:

```
led = LED(25)
```

Together, these two lines give Python the ability to control LEDs connected to Raspberry Pi's GPIO pins and tell it which pin – or pins, if you have more than one LED in your circuit – to control. To actually control the LED, type the following:

```
led.on()
```

To switch the LED off again, type:

```
led.off()
```

Congratulations, you now have control over your Raspberry Pi's GPIO pins in Python! Try typing those two instructions again. If the LED is already off, **led.off()** won't do anything; the same is true if the LED is already on and you type **led.on()**.

To make a true program, type the following into the script area:

```
from gpiozero import LED
from time import sleep

led = LED(25)

while True:
    led.on()
    sleep(1)
    led.off()
    sleep(1)
```

This program imports the LED function from the **gpiozero** (GPIO Zero) library and the **sleep** function from the **time** library, then constructs an infinite loop to turn the LED on for a second, turn it off for a second, and to repeat. Click the Run button to see it in action: your LED will begin to flash. As with the Scratch program, make a note of the behaviour when you click the Stop button while the LED is on versus while the LED is off.

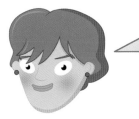

CHALLENGE: LONGER LIGHT-UP

How would you change the program to make the LED stay on for longer? What about staying off for longer? What's the smallest delay you can use while still seeing the LED switch on and off?

Using a breadboard

The next projects in this chapter will be much easier to complete if you're using a breadboard to hold the components and make the electrical connections.

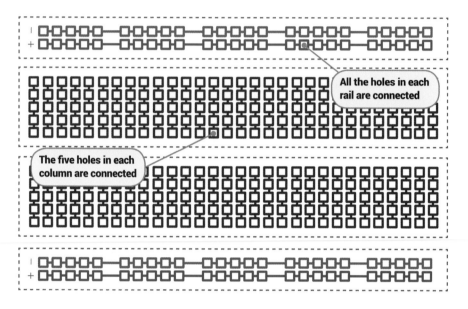

A breadboard is covered with holes – spaced, to match components, 2.54 mm apart. Under these holes are metal strips which act like the jumper wires you've been using until now. These run in rows across the board, with most boards having a gap down the middle to split them in two halves. Many breadboards also have letters across the top and numbers down the sides. These allow you to find a particular hole: A1 is the top-left corner, B1 is the hole to the immediate right, while B2 is one hole down from there. A1 is connected to B1 by the hidden metal strips, but no 1 hole is ever connected to any 2 hole unless you add a jumper wire yourself.

Larger breadboards also have strips of holes down the sides, typically marked with red and black or red and blue stripes. These are the *power rails*, and are designed to make wiring easier: you can connect a single wire from Raspberry Pi's ground pin to one of the power rails – typically marked with a blue or black stripe and a minus symbol – to provide a *common ground* for lots of components on the breadboard, and you can do the same if your circuit needs 3.3 V or 5 V power.

Adding electronic components to a breadboard is simple: just line their leads (the sticky-out metal parts) up with the holes and gently push until the component is in place. For connections you need to make beyond those the breadboard makes for you, you can use male-to-male (M2M) jumper wires; for connections from the breadboard to Raspberry Pi, use male-to-female (M2F) jumper wires.

Never try to cram more than one component lead or jumper wire into a single hole on the breadboard. Remember: holes are connected in columns, aside from the split in the middle, so a component lead in A1 is electrically connected to anything you add to B1, C1, D1, and E1.

Next steps: reading a button

Outputs like LEDs are one thing, but the 'input/output' part of 'GPIO' means you can use pins as inputs too. For this project, you'll need a breadboard, male-to-male (M2M) and male-to-female (M2F) jumper wires, and a push-button switch. If you don't have a breadboard you can use female-to-female (F2F) jumper wires, but the button will be much harder to press without accidentally breaking the circuit.

Start by adding the push-button to your breadboard. If your push-button has only two legs, make sure they're in different numbered rows of the breadboard; if it has four legs, turn it so the sides the legs come out from are along the breadboard's rows and the flat leg-free sides are at the top and bottom. Connect the ground rail of your breadboard to a ground pin of Raspberry Pi (marked GND on **Figure 6-4**) with a male-to-female jumper wire, then connect one leg of your push-button to the ground rail with a male-to-male jumper wire. Finally, connect the other leg – the one on the same side as the leg you just connected, if using a four-leg switch – to the GPIO 2 pin (marked GP2 on **Figure 6-4**) of Raspberry Pi with a male-to-female jumper wire.

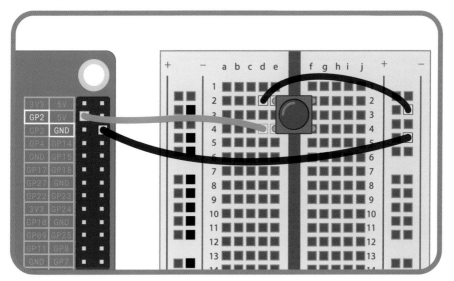

▲ **Figure 6-4:** Wiring a push-button to the GPIO pins

Reading a button in Scratch

Start a new Scratch program and drag a `when ⚑ clicked` block onto the code area. Connect a `set gpio to input pulled high` block, and select the number 2 from the drop-down to match the GPIO pin you used for the push-button.

If you click the green flag now, nothing will happen. That's because you've told Scratch to use the pin as an input, but not what to do with that input. Drag a `forever` block to the end of your sequence, then drag an `if then else` block inside it. Find the `gpio is high?` block, drag it into the diamond-shaped white space in the `if then` part of the block, and use the drop-down to select the number 2 to tell it which GPIO pin to check. Drag a `say hello! for 2 seconds` block into the `else` part of the block and edit it to say 'Button pushed!'. Leave the 'if then' part of the block empty for now.

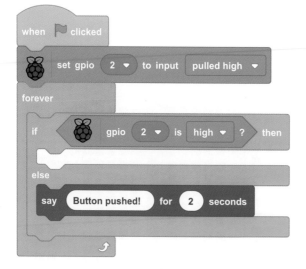

There's a lot going on there, but start by testing it: click the green flag, then push the button on your breadboard. Your sprite should tell you that the button has been pushed: you've successfully read an input from the GPIO pin!

You may have noticed that the `if gpio 2 is high? then` part of the block is empty. The code that runs when the button is actually pushed, meanwhile is in the `else` part of the block. That seems confusing, as surely pressing the button makes it go high? In fact, it's the opposite in this particular case: we have pulled the GPIO pin high by default, and pushing the button pulls it down to low.

Look at your circuit again: see how the button is connected to the GPIO 2 pin, which is providing the positive part of the circuit, and the ground pin. When the button is pushed, the voltage on the GPIO pin is pulled low through the ground pin, and your Scratch program stops running the code in your `if gpio 2 is high? then` block and instead runs the code in the `else` part of the block.

If that all sounds perplexing, just remember this: when a button is pushed, the pin goes low. Note that this is the case due to the design of this particular circuit.

To extend your program further, add the LED and resistor back into the circuit: remember to connect the resistor to the GPIO 25 pin and the long leg of the LED, and the shorter leg of the LED to the ground rail on your breadboard.

Drag the `say Button pushed! for 2 seconds` block off the code area to the block palette to delete it, then replace it with a `set gpio 25 to output high` block – remembering that you'll have to change the GPIO number using the drop-down arrow. Add a `set gpio 25 to output low` block – remembering to change the values – to the currently empty `if gpio 2 is high? then` part of the block.

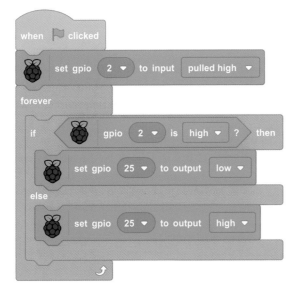

Click the green flag and push the button. The LED will light up as long as you're holding the button down; let go, and it will go dark again. Congratulations: you're controlling one GPIO pin based on an input from another!

CHALLENGE: MAKE IT STAY LIT

How would you change the program to make the LED stay on for a few seconds, even after you let go of the button? What would you need to change to have the LED on while you're not pressing the button and off while you are?

Reading a button in Python

Click the New button in Thonny to start a new project, and the Save button to save it as **Button Input**. Using a GPIO pin as an input for a button is very similar to using a pin as an output for an LED, but you need to import a different part of the GPIO Zero library. Type the following into the script area:

```
from gpiozero import Button
button = Button(2)
```

To have code run when the button is pressed, GPIO Zero provides the **wait_for_press** function. Type the following:

```
button.wait_for_press()
print("You pushed me!")
```

Click the Run button, then press the push-button switch. Your message will print to the Python shell at the bottom of the Thonny window: you've successfully read an input from the GPIO pin! If you want to try your program again, you'll need to click the Run button again; because there's no loop in the program, it quits as soon as it has finished printing the message to the shell.

To extend your program further, add the LED and resistor back into the circuit if you haven't already done so: remember to connect the resistor to the GPIO 25 pin and the long leg of the LED, and the shorter leg of the LED to the ground rail on your breadboard.

To control an LED as well as read a button, you'll need to import both the **Button** and **LED** functions from the GPIO Zero library. You'll also need the **sleep** function from the **time** library. Go back to the top of your program, and type in the following as the new first two lines:

```
from gpiozero import LED
from time import sleep
```

Below the line **button = Button(2)**, type:

```
led = LED(25)
```

Delete the line **print("You pushed me!")** and replace it with:

```
led.on()
sleep(3)
led.off()
```

Your finished program should look like this:

```
from gpiozero import LED
from time import sleep
from gpiozero import Button

button = Button(2)
led = LED(25)
button.wait_for_press()
led.on()
sleep(3)
led.off()
```

Click the Run button, then press the push-button switch: the LED will come on for three seconds, then turn off again and the program will exit. Congratulations: you can control an LED using a button input in Python!

CHALLENGE: ADD A LOOP

How would you add a loop to make the program repeat instead of exiting after one button press? What would you need to change to have the LED on while you're not pressing the button and off while you are?

Make some noise: controlling a buzzer

LEDs are a great output device, but not much use if you're looking in the other direction. The solution: buzzers, which make a noise audible anywhere in the room. For this project you'll need a breadboard, male-to-female (M2F) jumper wires, and an active buzzer. If you don't have a breadboard, you can connect the buzzer using female-to-female (F2F) jumper wires instead.

An active buzzer can be treated exactly like an LED, in terms of circuitry and programming. Repeat the circuit you made for the LED, but replace the LED with the active buzzer and leave the resistor out, as the buzzer will need more current to work. Connect one leg of the buzzer to the GPIO 15 pin (labelled GP15 in **Figure 6-5**) and the other to the ground pin (labelled GND in the diagram) using your breadboard and male-to-female jumper wires.

If your buzzer has three legs, make sure the leg marked with a minus symbol (-) is connected to the ground pin, and the leg marked with 'S' or 'SIGNAL' is connected to GPIO 15, then connect the remaining leg – usually the middle leg – to the 3.3 V pin (labelled 3V3.)

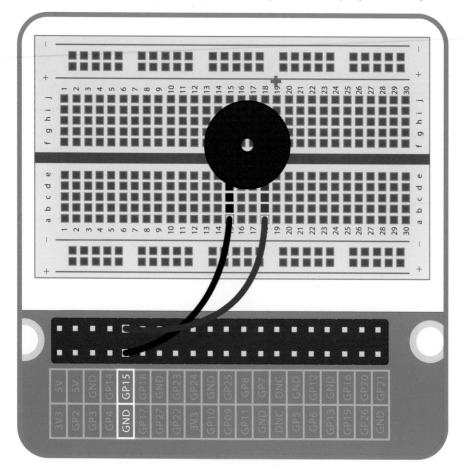

▲ **Figure 6-5:** Connecting a buzzer to the GPIO pins

Controlling a buzzer in Scratch

Recreate the same program as for making the LED flash – or load it, if you saved it before you created the button project. Use the drop-down in the `set gpio to output high` blocks to select number 15, so Scratch is controlling the correct GPIO pin.

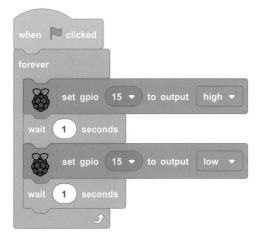

Click the green flag, and your buzzer will begin to buzz: one second on, and one second off. If you only hear the buzzer clicking once a second, you are using a passive buzzer rather than an active buzzer. Where an active buzzer generates the rapidly changing signal, known as an *oscillation*, to make the metal plates vibrate itself, a passive buzzer needs an oscillating signal. When you simply turn it on using Scratch, the plates only move once and stop – making the 'click' sound until the next time your program switches the pin on or off.

Click the red octagon to stop your buzzer, but make sure to do so when it's not making a sound, otherwise the buzzer will continue to buzz until you run your program again!

CHALLENGE: CHANGE THE BUZZ
How could you change the program to make the buzzer sound for a shorter time? Can you build a circuit so the buzzer is controlled by a button?

Controlling a buzzer in Python

Controlling an active buzzer through the GPIO Zero library is almost identical to controlling an LED, in that it has on and off states. You need a different, function, though: **buzzer**. Start a new project in Thonny and save it as **Buzzer**, then type the following:

```
from gpiozero import Buzzer
from time import sleep
```

As with LEDs, GPIO Zero needs to know which pin your buzzer is connected to in order to control it. Type the following:

```
buzzer = Buzzer(15)
```

From here, your program is almost identical to the one you wrote to control the LED; the only difference (apart from a different GPIO pin number) is you're using **buzzer** in place of **led**. Type the following:

```
while True:
    buzzer.on()
    sleep(1)
    buzzer.off()
    sleep(1)
```

Click the Run button and your buzzer will begin to buzz: one second on, and one second off. If you are using a passive buzzer rather than an active buzzer, you'll only hear a brief click every second instead of a continuous buzz: this is because a passive buzzer lacks an *oscillator* to create the rapidly changing signal which makes the plates inside the buzzer vibrate.

Click the Stop button to exit the program, but make sure the buzzer isn't making a sound at the time otherwise it will continue to buzz until you run your program again!

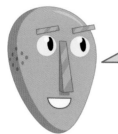

CHALLENGE: A BETTER BUZZ

How could you change the program to make the buzzer sound for a shorter time? Can you build a circuit so the buzzer is controlled by a button?

Scratch project: Traffic Lights

Now you know how to use buttons, buzzers, and LEDs as inputs and outputs, you're ready to build an example of real-world computing: traffic lights, complete with a button you can press to cross the road. For this project, you'll need a breadboard; a red, a yellow, and a green LED; three 330 Ω resistors; a buzzer; a push-button switch; and a selection of male-to-male (M2M) and male-to-female (M2F) jumper wires.

Start by building the circuit (**Figure 6-6**), connecting the buzzer to the GPIO 15 pin (labelled GP15 in **Figure 6-6**), the red LED to the GPIO 25 pin (labelled GP25), the yellow LED to GPIO 8 (GP8), the green LED to GPIO 7 (GP7), and the switch to GPIO 2 (GP2). Remember to connect the 330 Ω resistors between the GPIO pins and the long legs of the LEDs, and connect the second legs on all your components to the ground rail of your breadboard. Finally, connect the ground rail to a ground pin (labelled GND) on Raspberry Pi to complete the circuit.

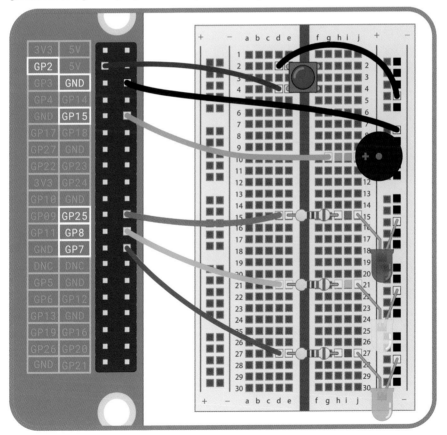

▲ **Figure 6-6:** Wiring diagram for the Traffic Lights project

Start a new Scratch 3 project, then drag a when 🏳 clicked block onto the code area. Next, you'll need to tell Scratch that the GPIO 2 pin, which is connected to the push-button switch in your circuit, is an input rather than an output: drag a `set gpio to input pulled high` block from the Raspberry Pi GPIO category of the blocks palette under your `when ⚐ clicked` block. Click on the down arrow next to '0' and select the number 2 from the drop-down list.

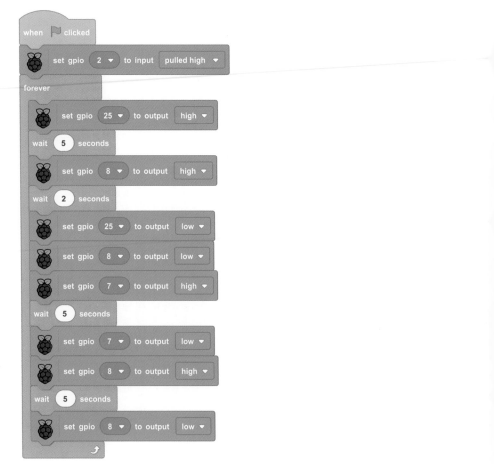

Next, you need to create your traffic light sequence. Drag a `forever` block into your program, then fill it with blocks to turn the traffic light LEDs on and off in a pattern. Remember which GPIO pins have which component attached: when you're using pin 25 you're using the red LED, pin 8 the yellow LED, and pin 7 the green LED.

Click the green flag, and watch your LEDs: first the red will light, then both the red and yellow, then the green, then the yellow, and finally the sequence repeats with the red light once more.

This pattern matches that used by traffic lights in the UK; you can edit the sequence to match patterns in other countries, if you wish.

To simulate a pedestrian crossing, you need your program to watch for the button being pressed. Click the red octagon to stop your program, if it's currently running. Drag an `if then else` block onto your script area and connect it so it's directly beneath your `forever` block, with your traffic light sequence in the 'if then' section. Leave the diamond-shaped gap empty for now.

A real pedestrian crossing doesn't change the light to red as soon as the button is pushed, but instead waits for the next red light in the sequence. To build that into your own program, drag a `when gpio is low` block onto the code area and select '2' from its drop-down list. Then drag a `set pushed to 1` block underneath it.

This block stack watches out for the button being pushed, then sets the variable 'pushed' to 1. Setting a variable this way lets you store the fact the button has been pushed, even though you're not going to act on it right away.

Go back to your original block stack and find the `if then` block. Drag a `○ = ○` Operator block into the `if then` block's diamond blank, then drag a `pushed` reporter block into the first blank space. Type '0' over the '50' on the right-hand side of the block.

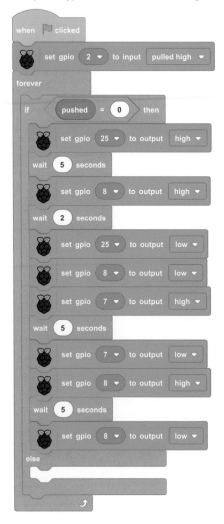

Click the green flag, and watch the traffic lights go through their sequence. Press the push-button switch: at first it will look like nothing is happening, but once the sequence has reached its end – with just the yellow LED lit – the traffic lights will go off and stay off, thanks to your 'pushed' variable.

All that's left to do is make your pedestrian crossing button actually do something other than turn the lights off. In the main block stack, find the else block and drag a set gpio 25 to output high block into it – remembering to change the default GPIO pin number to match the pin your red LED is connected to.

Beneath that, still in the else block, create a pattern for the buzzer. drag a repeat 10 block, then fill it with set gpio 15 to output high , wait 0.2 seconds , set gpio 15 to output low , and wait 0.2 seconds blocks, changing the GPIO pin values to match the pin for the buzzer component.

Finally, beneath the bottom of your repeat 10 block but still in the else block, add a set gpio 25 to output low block and a set pushed to 0 block – the last block resetting the variable that stores the button press, so the buzzer sequence doesn't just repeat forever.

Click the green flag, then push the switch on your breadboard. After the sequence has completed, you'll see the red light go on and the buzzer sound to let pedestrians know it's safe to cross. After a couple of seconds, the buzzer will stop and the traffic light sequence will start again and continue until the next time you press the button.

Congratulations: you have programmed your own fully functional set of traffic lights, complete with pedestrian crossing!

CHALLENGE: CAN YOU IMPROVE IT?

Can you change the program to give the pedestrian longer to cross? Can you find information about other countries' traffic light patterns and reprogram your lights to match? How could you make the LEDs less bright?

Python project: Quick Reaction Game

Now you know how to use buttons and LEDs as inputs and outputs, you're ready to build an example of real-world computing: a two-player quick-reaction game, designed to see who has the fastest reaction times! For this project you'll need a breadboard, an LED and a 330 Ω resistor, two push-button switches, some male-to-female (M2F) jumper wires, and some male-to-male (M2M) jumper wires.

Start by building the circuit (**Figure 6-7**): connect the first switch at the left-hand side of your breadboard to the GPIO 14 pin (labelled GP14 in **Figure 6-7**), the second switch at the right-hand side of your breadbOard to the GPIO 15 pin (labelled GP15), the LED's longer leg to the 330 Ω resistor which then connects to the GPIO 4 pin (labelled GP4) of Raspberry Pi, and the second legs on all your components to your breadboard's ground rail. Finally, connect the ground rail to Raspberry Pi's ground pin (labelled GND).

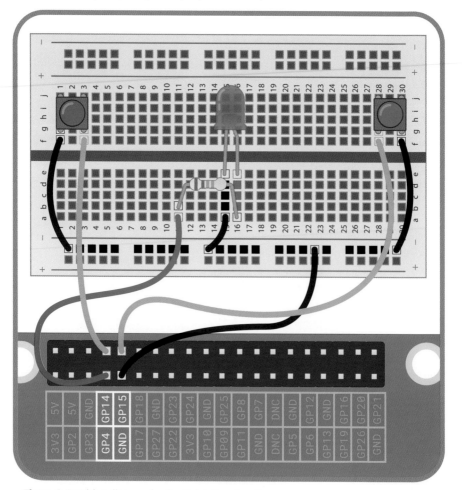

▲ **Figure 6-7:** Wiring diagram for the Quick Reaction Game

Start a new project in Thonny and save it as **Reaction Game**. You're going to be using the **LED** and **button** functions from the GPIO Zero library, and the `sleep` function from the time library. Rather than importing the two GPIO Zero functions on two separate lines, though, you can save time and import them together using a comma symbol (**,**) to separate them. Type the following in the script area:

```
from gpiozero import LED, Button
from time import sleep
```

As before, you'll need to tell GPIO Zero which pins the two buttons and the LED are connected to. Type the following:

```
led = LED(4)
right_button = Button(15)
left_button = Button(14)
```

Now add instructions to turn the LED on and off, so you can check it's working correctly:

```
led.on()
sleep(5)
led.off()
```

Click the Run button: the LED will turn on for five seconds, then turn off and the program will quit. For the purposes of a reaction game, though, having the LED go off after exactly 5 seconds every time is a bit predictable. Add the following below the line `from time import sleep`:

```
from random import uniform
```

The random library, as its name suggests, lets you generate random numbers (here with a uniform distribution – see **rpf.io/uniform**). Find the line `sleep(5)` and change it to read:

```
sleep(uniform(5, 10))
```

Click the Run button again: this time the LED will stay lit for a random number of seconds between 5 and 10. Count to see how long it takes for the LED to go off, then click the Run button a few more times: you'll see the time is different for each run, making the program less predictable.

To turn the buttons into triggers for each player, you'll need to add a function. Go to the very bottom of your program and type the following:

```
def pressed(button):
    print(str(button.pin.number) + " won the game")
```

Remember that Python uses indentation to know which lines are part of your function; Thonny will automatically indent the second line for you. Finally, add the following two lines to detect the players pressing the buttons – remembering that they must not be indented, or Python will treat them as part of your function.

```
right_button.when_pressed = pressed
left_button.when_pressed = pressed
```

Run your program, and this time try to press one of the two buttons as soon as the LED goes out. You'll see a message for the first button to be pushed printed to the Python shell at the bottom of the Thonny window. Unfortunately, you'll also see messages for each time either button is pushed – and they use the pin number rather than a friendly name for the button.

To fix that, start by asking the players for their names. Underneath the line **from random import uniform**, type the following:

```
left_name = input("Left player name is ")
right_name = input("Right player name is ")
```

Go back to your function and replace the line **print(str(button.pin.number) + " won the game")** with:

```
    if button.pin.number == 14:
        print (left_name + " won the game")
    else:
        print(right_name + " won the game")
```

Click the Run button, then type the names of both players into the Python shell area. When you press the button this time, remembering to do it as quickly as you can after the LED goes out, you'll see that the player name is printed instead of the pin number.

To fix the problem of all button presses being reported as having won, you'll need to add a new function from the sys – short for *system* – library: **exit**. Under the last **import** line, type the following:

```
from os import _exit
```

Then at the end of your function, under the line **print(right_name + " won the game")**, type the following:

```
    _exit(0)
```

The indentation is important here: **_exit(0)** should be indented by four spaces, lining up with **else:** two lines above it and **if** two lines above that. This instruction tells Python to stop the program after the first button is pressed, meaning the player whose button is pressed second doesn't get any reward for losing!

Your finished program should look like this:

```
from gpiozero import LED, Button
from time import sleep
from random import uniform
from os import _exit

left_name = input("Left player name is ")
right_name = input ("Right player name is ")
led = LED(4)
right_button = Button(15)
left_button = Button(14)

led.on()
sleep(uniform(5, 10))
led.off()

def pressed(button):
    if button.pin.number == 14:
        print(left_name + " won the game")
    else:
        print(right_name + " won the game")
    _exit(0)

right_button.when_pressed = pressed
left_button.when_pressed = pressed
```

Click the Run button, enter the players' names, wait for the LED to go off, and you'll see the name of the winning player. You'll also see a message from Python itself: **Backend terminated or disconnected . Use 'Stop/Restart' to restart ...** This simply means that Python received your **_exit(0)** command and halted the program, but that you'll need to click the Stop icon to fully quit and prepare your program for another round (**Figure 6-8**, overleaf).

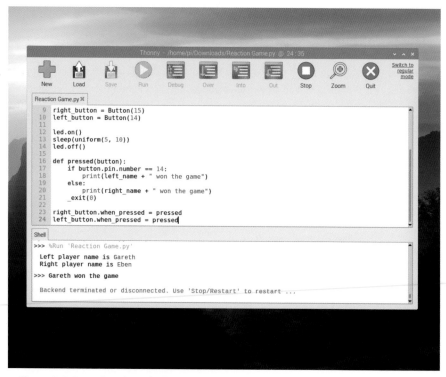

```
     9  right_button = Button(15)
    10  left_button = Button(14)
    11
    12  led.on()
    13  sleep(uniform(5, 10))
    14  led.off()
    15
    16  def pressed(button):
    17      if button.pin.number == 14:
    18          print(left_name + " won the game")
    19      else:
    20          print(right_name + " won the game")
    21          _exit(0)
    22
    23  right_button.when_pressed = pressed
    24  left_button.when_pressed = pressed
```

```
>>> %Run 'Reaction Game.py'
Left player name is Gareth
Right player name is Eben
>>> Gareth won the game

Backend terminated or disconnected. Use 'Stop/Restart' to restart ...
```

▲ **Figure 6-8:** Once the winner is decided, you'll need to stop the program

Congratulations: you've made your own physical game!

CHALLENGE: IMPROVE THE GAME

Can you add a loop, so the game runs continuously? Remember to remove the `_exit(0)` instruction first! Can you add a score counter, so you can see who is winning over multiple rounds? What about a timer, so you can see just how long it took you to react to the light going off?

Chapter 7

Physical computing with the Sense HAT

As used on the International Space Station, the Sense HAT is a multifunctional add-on board for Raspberry Pi, equipped with sensors and an LED matrix display

Raspberry Pi comes with support for a special type of add-on board called *Hardware Attached on Top (HAT)*. HATs can add everything from microphones and lights to electronic relays and screens to Raspberry Pi, but one HAT in particular is very special: the Sense HAT.

The Sense HAT was designed specially for the Astro Pi space mission. A joint project between the Raspberry Pi Foundation, UK Space Agency, and European Space Agency, Astro Pi saw Raspberry Pi boards and Sense HATs carried up to the International Space Station aboard an Orbital Science Cygnus cargo rocket. Since safely reaching orbit high above the Earth, the Sense HATs – nicknamed Ed and Izzy by the astronauts – have been used to run code and carry out scientific experiments contributed by schoolchildren from across Europe.

While Ed and Izzy are a little far away for you to use them yourself, the same Sense HAT hardware can be found here on Earth, too, at all Raspberry Pi retailers – and if you don't want to buy a Sense HAT right now, you can simulate one in software!

> **REAL OR SIMULATED**
>
> This chapter is best partnered with a real Sense HAT attached to a Raspberry Pi's GPIO header, but anyone who doesn't have one can skip the section titled 'Installing the Sense HAT' and simply try the projects out in the Sense HAT Emulator; they'll work just as well!

Introducing the Sense HAT

The Sense HAT is a powerful, multifunctional add-on for Raspberry Pi. As well as an 8×8 matrix of 64 red, green, and blue (RGB) programmable LEDs which can be controlled to produce any colour from a range of millions, the Sense HAT includes a five-way joystick controller and six on-board sensors.

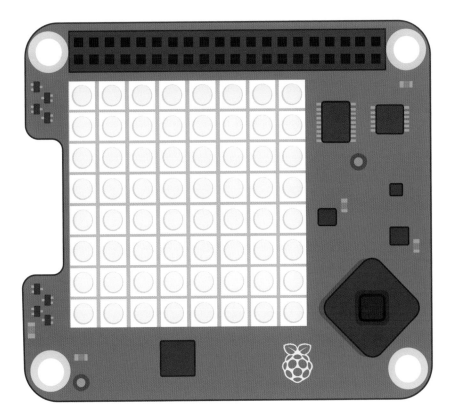

Gyroscope sensor: Used to sense changes in angle over time, technically known as *angular velocity*, by keeping track of the direction of Earth's gravity field – the force which pulls things down towards the centre of the planet. Put simply, the gyroscopic sensor can tell when you rotate the Sense HAT relative to the surface of the Earth and how quickly it's rotating.

Accelerometer: Similar to the gyroscope sensor, but rather than monitoring an angle relative to the Earth's gravity it measures acceleration force in multiple directions. Combined, readings (data) from the two sensors can help you track where a Sense HAT is pointing and how it's being moved.

Magnetometer: Measures the strength of a magnetic field, and is another sensor which can help track the Sense HAT's movements: by measuring the Earth's natural magnetic field, the magnetometer can figure out the direction of magnetic north. The same sensor can also be used to detect metallic objects, and even electrical fields. All three of these sensors are built into a single chip, labelled 'ACCEL/GYRO/MAG' on the Sense HAT's circuit board.

Humidity sensor: Measures the amount of water vapour in the air, known as the *relative humidity*. Relative humidity can range from 0%, for there being no water at all, to 100%, for the air being completely saturated. Humidity data can be used to detect when it might be about to rain!

Barometric pressure sensor: also known as the *barometer*, it measures air pressure. Although most people will be familiar with barometric pressure from the weather forecast, the barometer has a secret second use: it can track when you're climbing up or down a hill or mountain, as the air gets thinner and lower pressure the further you get from Earth's sea level.

Temperature sensor: Measures how hot or cold the surrounding environment is, though it is also affected by how hot or cold the Sense HAT is: if you're using a case, you may find your readings higher than you expect. The Sense HAT doesn't have a separate temperature sensor; instead, it uses temperature sensors built into the humidity and barometric pressure sensors. A program can use one or both of these sensors; it's up to you.

Installing the Sense HAT

If you have a physical Sense HAT, start by unpacking it and making sure you have all the pieces: you should have the Sense HAT itself, four metal or plastic pillars known as *spacers*, and eight screws. You may also have some metal pins in a black plastic strip, like the GPIO pins on Raspberry Pi; if so, push this strip pin-side-up through the bottom of the Sense HAT until you hear a click.

The spacers are designed to stop the Sense HAT from bending and flexing as you use the joystick. While the Sense HAT will work without them being installed, using them will help protect your Sense HAT, Raspberry Pi, and GPIO header from being damaged.

> **WARNING!**
> Hardware Attached on Top (HAT) modules should only ever be plugged into and removed from the GPIO header while your Raspberry Pi is switched off and disconnected from its power supply. Always be careful to keep the HAT flat when installing it, and double-check it is lined up with the GPIO header pins before pushing it down.

Install the spacers by pushing four of the screws up from underneath the bottom of Raspberry Pi through the four mounting holes at each corner, then twist the spacers onto the screws. Push the Sense HAT down onto Raspberry Pi's GPIO header, making sure to line it up properly with the pins underneath and to keep it as flat as possible. Finally, screw the final four screws through the mounting holes on the Sense HAT and into the spacers you installed earlier. If it's installed properly, the Sense HAT should be flat and level and shouldn't bend or wobble as you push on its joystick.

Plug the power back into your Raspberry Pi, and you'll see the LEDs on the Sense HAT light up in a rainbow pattern (**Figure 7-1**), then switch off again. Your Sense HAT is now installed!

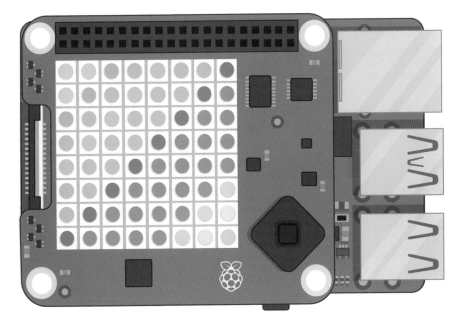

▲ **Figure 7-1:** A rainbow pattern appears when the power is first turned on

If you want to remove the Sense HAT again, simply undo the top screws, lift the HAT off – being careful not to bend the pins on the GPIO header, as the HAT holds on quite tightly (you may need to prise it off with a small screwdriver) – then remove the spacers from Raspberry Pi.

Hello, Sense HAT!

As with all programming projects, there's an obvious place to start with the Sense HAT: scrolling a welcome message across its LED display. If you're using the Sense HAT emulator, load it now by clicking on the Raspbian menu icon, choosing the Programming category, and clicking on Sense HAT Emulator.

PROGRAMMING EXPERIENCE

This chapter assumes experience with Scratch 3 or Python and the Thonny integrated development environment (IDE), depending on if you're working through the Scratch or Python code examples – or both! If you haven't done so already, please turn to **Chapter 4, Programming with Scratch**, or **Chapter 5, Programming with Python**, and work through the projects in that chapter first.

Greetings from Scratch

Load Scratch 3 from the Raspbian menu, then click on the Add Extension button at the bottom-left of the Scratch window. Click on the Raspberry Pi Sense HAT extension (**Figure 7-2**). This loads the blocks you need to control the various features of the Sense HAT, including its LED display. When you need them, you'll find them in the Raspberry Pi Sense HAT category.

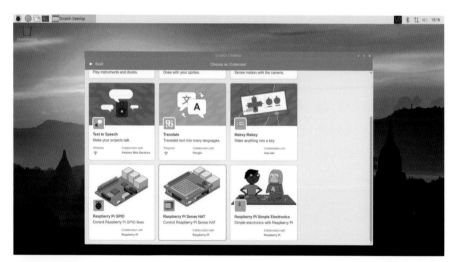

▲ **Figure 7-2:** Adding the Raspberry Pi Sense HAT extension to Scratch 3

Start by dragging a `when ⚑ clicked` Events block onto the script area, then drag a `display text Hello!` block directly underneath it. Edit the text so that the block reads `display text Hello, World!`.

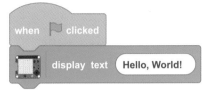

Click the green flag on the stage area and watch your Sense HAT or the Sense HAT emulator: the message will scroll slowly across Sense HAT's LED matrix, lighting up the LED pixels to form each letter in turn (**Figure 7-3**). Congratulations: your program's a success!

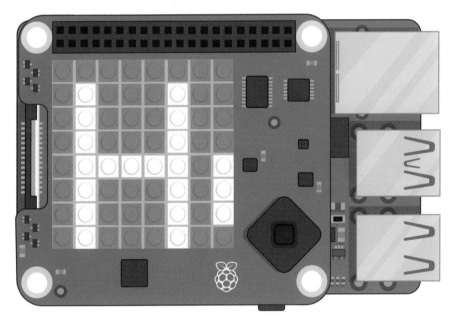

▲ **Figure 7-3**: Your message scrolls across the LED matrix

Now you can scroll a simple message, it's time to take a look at controlling how that message is displayed As well as being able to modify the message to be displayed, you can alter the rotation – which way the message is displayed on the Sense HAT. Drag a set rotation to 0 degrees block from the blocks palette and insert it below when ⚑ clicked and above display text Hello, World!, then click on the down arrow next to 0 and change it to 90. Click the green flag and you'll see the same message as before, but rather than scrolling left-to-right it will scroll bottom-to-top (**Figure 7-4**, overleaf) – you'll need to turn your head, or the Sense HAT, to read it!

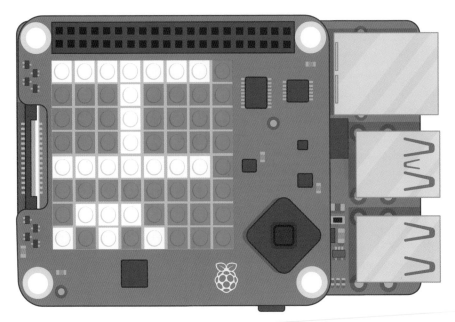

▲ **Figure 7-4:** This time the message scrolls vertically

Now change the rotation back to 0, then drag a `set colour` block between `set rotation to 0 degrees` and `display text Hello, World!`. Click on the colour at the end of the block to bring up Scratch's colour picker and find a nice bright yellow colour, then click the green flag to see how your program's output has changed (**Figure 7-5**).

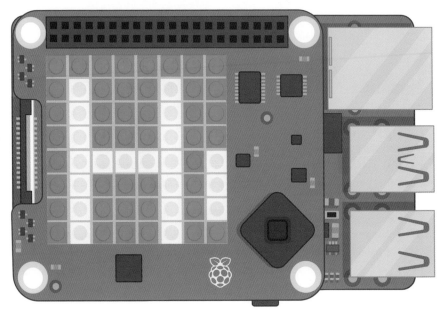

▲ **Figure 7-5:** Changing the colour of the text

Finally, drag a `set background` block between `set colour to yellow` and `display text Hello, World!`, then click on the colour to bring up the colour picker again. This time, choosing a colour doesn't affect the LEDs that make up the message but the LEDs that don't – known as the background. Find a nice blue colour, then click the green flag again: this time your message will be in a bright yellow on a blue background. Try changing these colours to find your favourite combination – not all colours work well together!

As well as being able to scroll entire messages, you can show individual letters. Drag your `display text` block off the script area to delete it, then drag a `display character A` block onto the script area in its place. Click the green flag, and you'll see the difference: this block shows only one letter at a time, and the letter stays on the Sense HAT until you tell it otherwise without scrolling or disappearing. The same colour control blocks apply to this block as the `display text` block: try changing the letter's colour to red (**Figure 7-6**).

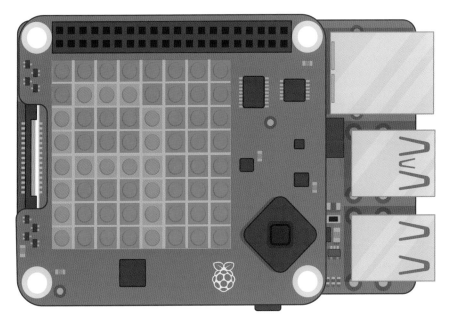

▲ **Figure 7-6:** Displaying a single letter

CHALLENGE: REPEAT THE MESSAGE

Can you use your knowledge of loops to have a scrolling message repeat itself? Can you make a program that spells out a word letter-by-letter using different colours?

Greetings from Python

Load Thonny by clicking on the Raspbian menu icon, choosing Programming, and clicking on Thonny. If you're using the Sense HAT emulator and it gets covered by the Thonny window, click and hold the mouse button on either window's title bar – at the top, in blue – and drag it to move it around the desktop until you can see both windows.

PYTHON LINE CHANGE

Python code written for a physical Sense HAT runs on the Sense HAT emulator, and vice-versa, with only one change. If you're using the Sense HAT emulator with Python you'll need to change the line from `sense_hat import SenseHat` in all the programs from this chapter to `from sense_emu import SenseHat` instead. If you want to then run them on a physical Sense HAT again, just change the line back!

To use the Sense HAT, or Sense HAT emulator, in a Python program, you need to import the Sense HAT library. Type the following into the script area, remembering to use **sense_emu** (in place of **sense_hat**) if you're using the Sense HAT emulator:

```
from sense_hat import SenseHat
sense = SenseHat()
```

The Sense HAT library has a simple function for taking a message, formatting it so that it can be shown on the LED display, and scrolling it smoothly. Type the following:

```
sense.show_message("Hello, World!")
```

Save your program as **Hello Sense HAT**, then click the Run button. You'll see your message scroll slowly across the Sense HAT's LED matrix, lighting up the LED pixels to form each letter in turn (**Figure 7-7**). Congratulations: your program's a success!

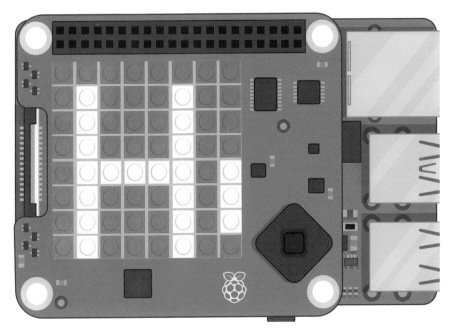

▲ **Figure 7-7:** Scrolling a message across the LED matrix

The **show_message()** function has more tricks up its sleeve than that, though. Go back to your program and edit the last line so it says:

```
sense.show_message("Hello, World!", text_colour=(255, 255, 0),
back_colour=(0, 0, 255), scroll_speed=(0.05))
```

These extra instructions, separated by commas, are known as *parameters*, and they control various aspects of the **show_message()** function. The simplest is **scroll_speed=()**, which changes how quickly the message scrolls across the screen. A value of 0.05 in here scrolls at roughly twice the usual speed. The bigger the number, the lower the speed.

The **text_colour=()** and **back_colour=()** parameters – spelled in the British English way, unlike most Python instructions – set the colour of the writing and the background respectively. They don't accept names of colours, though; you have to state the colour you want as a trio of numbers. The first number represents the amount of red in the colour, from 0 for no red at all to 255 for as much red as possible; the second number is the amount of green in the colour; and the third number the amount of blue. Together, these are known as *RGB* – for red, green, and blue.

Click on the Run icon and watch the Sense HAT: this time, the message will scroll considerably more quickly, and be in a bright yellow on a blue background (**Figure 7-8**, overleaf). Try changing the parameters to find a speed and colour combination that works for you.

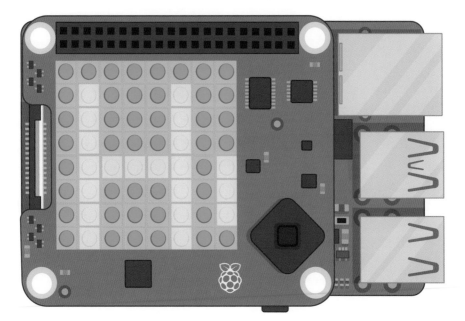

If you want to use friendly names instead of RGB values to set your colours, you'll need to create variables. Above your **sense.show_message()** line, add the following:

```
yellow = (255, 255, 0)
blue = (0, 0, 255)
```

Go back to your **sense.show_message()** line and edit it so it reads:

```
sense.show_message("Hello, World!", text_colour=(yellow), back_
colour=(blue), scroll_speed=(0.05))
```

Click the Run icon again, and you'll see nothing has changed: your message is still in yellow on a blue background. This time, though, you've used the variable names to make your code more readable: instead of a string of numbers, the code explains what colour it's setting. You can define as many colours as you like: try adding a variable called 'red' with the values 255, 0, and 0; a variable called 'white' with the values 255, 255, 255; and a variable called 'black' with the values 0, 0, and 0.

As well as being able to scroll full messages, you can display individual letters. Delete your **sense.show_message()** line altogether, and type the following in its place:

```
sense.show_letter("Z")
```

Click Run, and you'll see the letter 'Z' appear on the Sense HAT's display. This time, it'll stay there: individual letters, unlike messages, don't automatically scroll. You can control `sense.show_letter()` with the same colour parameters as `sense.show_message()`, too: try changing the colour of the letter to red (**Figure 7-9**).

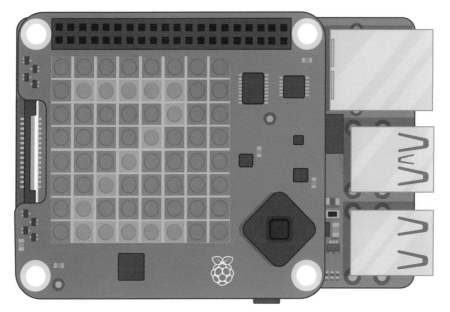

▲ **Figure 7-9:** Displaying a single letter

CHALLENGE: REPEAT THE MESSAGE

Can you use your knowledge of loops have a scrolling message repeat itself? Can you make a program that spells out a word letter-by-letter using different colours? How fast can you make a message scroll?

Next steps: **Drawing with light**

The Sense HAT's LED display isn't just for messages: you can display pictures, too. Each LED can be treated as a single pixel – short for *picture element* – in an image of your choosing, allowing you to jazz up your programs with pictures and even animation.

To create drawings, though, you need to be able to change individual LEDs. To do that, you'll need to understand how the Sense HAT's LED matrix is laid out in order to write a program that turns the correct LEDs on or off.

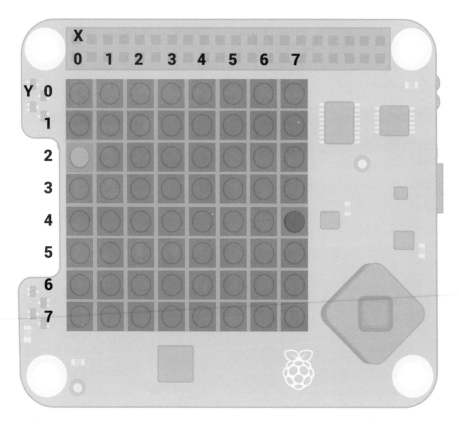

▲ **Figure 7-10:** LED matrix coordinates system

There are eight LEDs in each row of the display, and eight in each column (**Figure 7-10**). When counting the LEDs, though, you – like most programming languages – should start at 0 and end at 7. The first LED is in the top-left corner, the last is in the bottom right. Using the numbers from the rows and columns, you can find the *coordinates* of any LED on the matrix. The blue LED in the pictured matrix is at coordinates 0, 2; the red LED is at coordinates 7, 4. The X axis, across the matrix, comes first, followed by the Y axis, down the matrix.

When planning pictures to draw on the Sense HAT, it may help to draw them by hand first, on gridded paper, or you can plan things out in a spreadsheet such as LibreOffice Calc.

Pictures in Scratch

Start a new project in Scratch, saving your existing project if you want to keep it. If you've been working through the projects in this chapter, Scratch 3 will keep the Raspberry Pi Sense HAT extension loaded; if you have closed and reopened Scratch 3 since your last project, load the extension using the Add Extension button. Drag a `when ⚑ clicked` Events block onto the code area, then drag `set background` and `set colour` blocks underneath it. Edit both to set the background colour to black and the colour to white: make black by sliding the Brightness and Saturation sliders to 0; make white by sliding Brightness to 100 and Saturation to 0. You'll need to do this at the start of every Sense HAT program, otherwise Scratch will simply use the last colours you chose – even if you chose them in a different program. Finally, drag a `display raspberry` block to the bottom of your program.

Click the green flag: you'll see the Sense HAT's LEDs light up a raspberry (**Figure 7-11**).

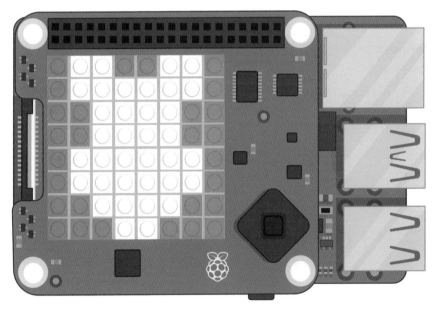

▲ **Figure 7-11:** Don't look directly at the LEDs when they're bright white

You're not limited to the preset raspberry shape, either. Click on the down-arrow next to the raspberry to activated drawing mode: you can click on any LED on the pattern to switch it on or off, while the two buttons at the bottom set all LEDs to off or on. Try drawing your own pattern now, then click the green arrow to see it on the Sense HAT. Also try changing the colour and the background colour using the blocks above.

When you've finished, drag the three blocks into the blocks palette to delete them, and place a `clear display` block under `when ⚑ clicked`; click the green flag, and all the LEDs will switch off.

To make a picture, you need to be able to control individual pixels and to give them different colours. You can do this by chaining edited (display raspberry) blocks with (set colour) blocks, or you can address each pixel individually. To create your own version of the LED matrix example pictured at the start of this section, with two specifically selected LEDs lit up in red and blue, leave the (clear display) block at the top of your program and drag a (set background) block underneath it. Change the (set background) block to black, then drag two (set pixel x 0 y 0) blocks underneath it. Finally, edit these blocks as follows:

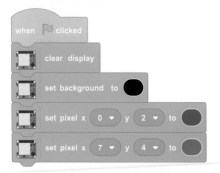

Click the green flag, and you'll see your LEDs light up to match the matrix image (**Figure 7-10**) on page 158. Congratulations: you can control individual LEDs!

Edit your existing set pixel blocks as follows, and drag more onto the bottom until you have the following program:

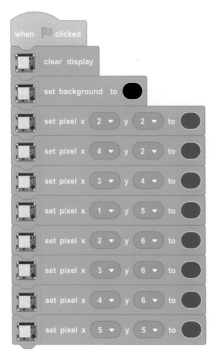

Before you click the green flag, see if you can guess what picture is going to appear based on the LED matrix coordinates you've used, then run your program and see if you're right!

CHALLENGE: NEW DESIGNS

Can you design more pictures? Try getting some graph or grid paper and using it to plan out your picture by hand first. Can you draw a picture and have the colours change?

Pictures in Python

Start a new program in Thonny and save it as Sense HAT Drawing, then type the following – remembering to use **sense_emu** (in place of **sense_hat**) if you're using the emulator.

```
from sense_hat import SenseHat
sense = SenseHat()
```

Remember that you need both these lines your program in order to use the Sense HAT. Next, type:

```
sense.clear(255, 255, 255)
```

While not looking directly at the Sense HAT's LEDs, click the Run icon: you should see them all turn a bright white (**Figure 7-12**, overleaf) – which is why you shouldn't be looking directly at them when you run your program!

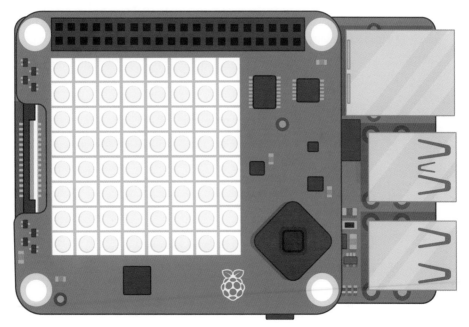

▲ **Figure 7-12:** Don't look directly at the matrix when it's lit up in bright white

The **sense.clear()** is designed to clear the LEDs of any previous programming, but accepts RGB colour parameters – meaning you can change the display to any colour you like. Try editing the line to:

```
sense.clear(0, 255, 0)
```

Click Run, and the Sense HAT will go bright green (**Figure 7-13**). Experiment with different colours, or add the colour-name variables you created for your Hello World program to make things easier to read.

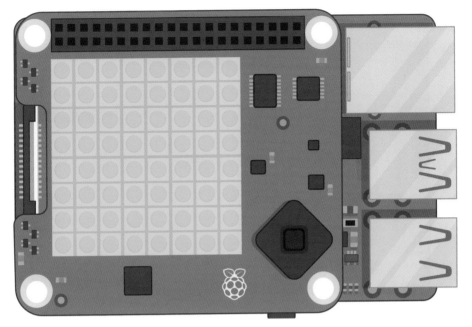

▲ **Figure 7-13:** The LED matrix lit up in bright green

To clear the LEDs, you need to use the RGB values for black: 0 red, 0 blue, and 0 green. There's an easier way, though. Edit the line of your program to read:

```
sense.clear()
```

The Sense HAT will go dark; for the **sense.clear()** function, having nothing between the brackets is equivalent to telling it to turn all LEDS to black – i.e. switch them off (**Figure 7-14**, overleaf). When you need to completely clear the LEDs in your programs, that's the function to use.

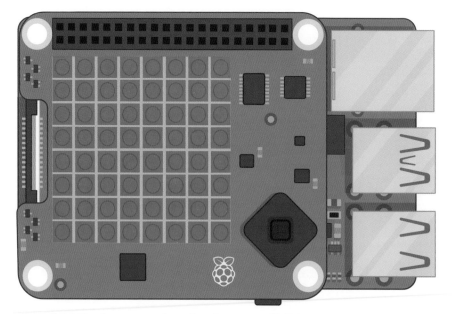

▲ **Figure 7-14:** Use the `sense.clear` function to turn off all the LEDs

To create your own version of the LED matrix pictured earlier in this chapter, with two specifically selected LEDs lit up in red and blue, add the following lines to your program after `sense.clear()`:

```
sense.set_pixel(0, 2, (0, 0, 255))
sense.set_pixel(7, 4, (255, 0, 0))
```

The first pair of numbers are the pixel's location on the matrix, X (across) axis followed by Y (down) axis. The second, in their own set of brackets, are the RGB values for pixel's colour. Click the Run button and you'll see the effect: two LEDs on your Sense HAT will light up, just like in **Figure 7-10** on page 164.

Delete those two lines, and type in the following:

```
sense.set_pixel(2, 2, (0, 0, 255))
sense.set_pixel(4, 2, (0, 0, 255))
sense.set_pixel(3, 4, (100, 0, 0))
sense.set_pixel(1, 5, (255, 0, 0))
sense.set_pixel(2, 6, (255, 0, 0))
sense.set_pixel(3, 6, (255, 0, 0))
sense.set_pixel(4, 6, (255, 0, 0))
sense.set_pixel(5, 5, (255, 0, 0))
```

Before you click Run, look at the coordinates and compare them to the matrix: can you guess what picture those instructions are going to draw? Click Run to find out if you're right!

Drawing a detailed picture using individual **set_pixel()** functions is slow, though. To speed things up, you can change multiple pixels at the same time. Delete all your **set_pixel()** lines and type the following:

```
g = (0, 255, 0)
b = (0, 0, 0)

creeper_pixels = [
    g, g, g, g, g, g, g, g,
    g, g, g, g, g, g, g, g,
    g, b, b, g, g, b, b, g,
    g, b, b, g, g, b, b, g,
    g, g, g, b, b, g, g, g,
    g, g, b, b, b, b, g, g,
    g, g, b, b, b, b, g, g,
    g, g, b, g, g, b, g, g
]

sense.set_pixels(creeper_pixels)
```

There's a lot there, but start by clicking Run to see if you recognise a certain little creeper. The first two lines create two variables to hold colours: green and black. To make the code for the drawing easier to write and read, the variables are single letters: 'g' for green and 'b' for black.

The next block of code creates a variable which holds colour values for all 64 pixels on the LED matrix, separated by commas and enclosed between square brackets. Instead of numbers, though, it uses the colour variables you created earlier: look closely, remembering 'g' is for green and 'b' is for black, and you can already see the picture that will appear (**Figure 7-15**, overleaf).

Finally, **sense.set_pixels(creeper_pixels)** takes that variable and uses the **sense.set_pixels()** function to draw on the entire matrix at once. Much easier than trying to draw pixel-by-pixel!

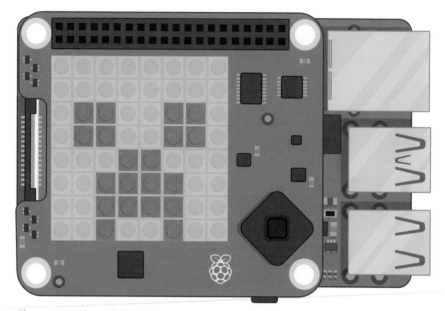

▲ **Figure 7-15:** Displaying an image on the matrix

You can also rotate and flip images, either as a way to show images the right way up when your Sense HAT is turned around or as a way of creating simple animations from a single asymmetrical image.

Start by editing your **creeper_pixels** variable to close his left eye, by replacing the four 'b' pixels, starting with the first two on the third line and then the first two on the fourth line, with 'g':

```
creeper_pixels = [
    g, g, g, g, g, g, g, g,
    g, g, g, g, g, g, g, g,
    g, g, g, g, g, b, b, g,
    g, g, g, g, g, b, b, g,
    g, g, g, b, b, g, g, g,
    g, g, b, b, b, b, g, g,
    g, g, b, b, b, b, g, g,
    g, g, b, g, g, b, g, g
]
```

Click Run, and you'll see the creeper's left eye close (**Figure 7-16**). To make an animation, go to the top of your program and add the line:

```
from time import sleep
```

Then go to the bottom and type:

```
while True:
    sleep(1)
    sense.flip_h()
```

Click Run, and watch the creeper as it closes and opens its eyes, one at a time!

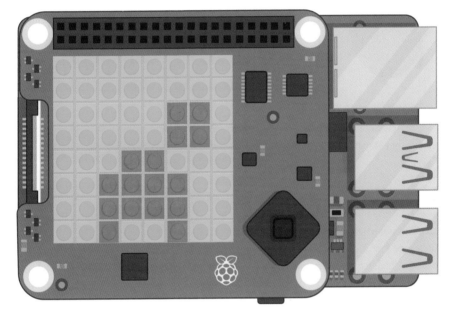

▲ **Figure 7-16:** Showing a simple two-frame animation

The **flip_h()** function flips an image on the horizontal axis, across; if you want to flip an image on its vertical axis, replace **sense.flip_h()** with **sense.flip_v()** instead. You can also rotate an image by 0, 90, 180, or 270 degrees using **sense.set_rotation(90)**, changing the number according to how many degrees you want to rotate the image. Try using this to have the creeper spin around instead of blinking!

CHALLENGE: NEW DESIGNS

Can you design more pictures and animations? Try getting some graph or grid paper and using it to plan out your picture by hand, first, to make writing the variable easier. Can you draw a picture and have the colours change? Tip: you can change the variables after you've already used them once.

Sensing the world around you

The Sense HAT's real power lies in the various sensors it has. These allow you to take readings of everything from temperature to acceleration, and use them in your programs as you see fit.

EMULATING THE SENSORS

If you're using the Sense HAT Emulator, you'll need to enable inertial and environmental sensor simulation: in the Emulator, click Edit, then Preferences, then tick them. In the same menu choose '180°..360°|0°..180°' under 'Orientation Scale' to make sure the numbers in the Emulator match the numbers reported by Scratch and Python, then click the Close button.

Environmental Sensing

The barometric pressure sensor, humidity sensor, and temperature sensor are all environmental sensors; they take measurements from the environment surrounding the Sense HAT.

Environmental sensing in Scratch

Start a new program in Scratch, saving your old one if you wish, and add the Raspberry Pi Sense HAT extension if it isn't already loaded. Drag a `when ⚑ clicked` Events block onto your code area, then a `clear display` block underneath, and a `set background to black` block underneath that. Next, add a `set colour to white` block – use the Brightness and Saturation sliders to choose the correct colour. It's always a good idea to do this at the start of your programs, as it will make sure the Sense HAT isn't showing anything from an old program while guaranteeing what colours you're using.

Drag a `say Hello! for 2 seconds` Looks block directly underneath your existing blocks. To take a reading from the pressure sensor, find the `pressure` block in the Raspberry Pi Sense HAT category and drag it over the word 'Hello!' in your `say Hello! for 2 seconds` block.

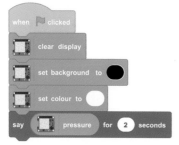

Click the green flag and the Scratch cat will tell you the current reading from the pressure sensor in *millibars*. After two seconds, the message will disappear; try blowing on the Sense HAT (or moving the Pressure slide up in the emulator) and clicking the green flag to run the program again; you should see a higher reading this time (**Figure 7-17**).

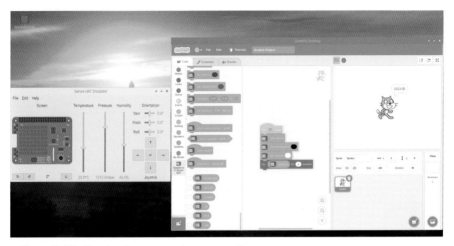

▲ **Figure 7-17:** Showing the pressure sensor reading

CHANGING VALUES

If you're using the Sense HAT emulator, you can change the values reported by each of the emulated sensors using its sliders and buttons. Try sliding the pressure sensor setting down towards the bottom, then clicking the green flag again.

To switch to the humidity sensor, delete the `pressure` block and replace it with `humidity`. Run your program again, and you'll see the current relative humidity of your room. Again, you can try running it again while blowing on the Sense HAT (or moving the emulator's Humidity slider up) to change the reading (**Figure 7-18**) – your breath is surprisingly humid!

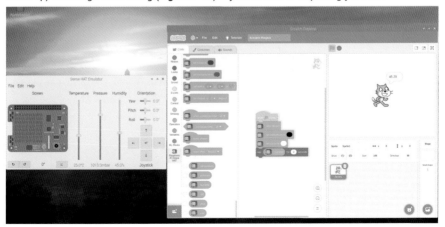

▲ **Figure 7-18:** Displaying the reading from the humidity sensor

For the temperature sensor, it's as easy as deleting the humidity block and replacing it with temperature, then running your program again. You'll see a temperature in degrees Celsius (**Figure 7-19**). This might not be the exact temperature of your room, however. Raspberry Pi generates heat all the time it's running, and this warms the Sense HAT and its sensors too.

▲ **Figure 7-19:** Displaying the temperature sensor reading

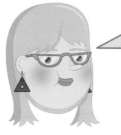

CHALLENGE: SCROLL & LOOP

Can you change your program to take a reading from each of the sensors in turn, then scroll them across the LED matrix rather than printing them to the stage area? Can you make your program loop, so it's constantly printing the current environmental conditions?

Environmental sensing in Python

To start taking readings from sensors, create a new program in Thonny and save it as **Sense HAT Sensors**. Type the following into the script area, as you always should when using the Sense HAT – and remember to use **sense_emu** if you're using the emulator.

```
from sense_hat import SenseHat
sense = SenseHat()
sense.clear()
```

It's always a good idea to include **sense.clear()** at the start of your programs, just in case the Sense HAT's display is still showing something from the last program it ran.

To take a reading from the pressure sensor, type:

```
pressure = sense.get_pressure()
print(pressure)
```

Click Run and you'll see a number printed to the Python shell at the bottom of the Thonny window. This is the air pressure reading detected by the barometric pressure sensor, in *millibars* (**Figure 7-20**). Try blowing on the Sense HAT (or moving the Pressure slider up in the emulator) while clicking the Run icon again; the number should be higher this time.

▲ **Figure 7-20:** Printing a pressure reading from the Sense HAT

CHANGING VALUES

If you're using the Sense HAT emulator, you can change the values reported by each of the emulated sensors using its sliders and buttons. Try sliding the pressure sensor setting down towards the bottom, then clicking Run again.

To switch to the humidity sensor, remove the last two lines of code and replace them with:

```
humidity = sense.get_humidity()
print(humidity)
```

Click Run and you'll see another number printed to the Python shell: this time, it's the current relative humidity of your room as a percentage. Again, you can blow on the Sense HAT (or move the emulator's Humidity slider up) and you'll see it go up when you run your program again (**Figure 7-21**, overleaf)– your breath is surprisingly humid!

▲ **Figure 7-21:** Displaying the humidity sensor reading

For the temperature sensor, remove the last two lines of your program and replace them with:

```
temp = sense.get_temperature()
print(temp)
```

Click Run again, and you'll see a temperature in degrees Celsius (**Figure 7-22**). This might not be the exact temperature of your room, however. Raspberry Pi generates heat all the time it's running, and this warms the Sense HAT and its sensors too.

▲ **Figure 7-22:** Showing the current temperature reading

Normally the Sense HAT reports the temperature based on a reading from the temperature sensor built into the humidity sensor; if you want to use the reading from the pressure sensor instead, you should use **sense.get_temperature_from_pressure()**. It's also possible to combine the two readings to get an average, which may be more accurate than using either sensor alone. Delete the last two lines of your program and type:

```
htemp = sense.get_temperature()
ptemp = sense.get_temperature_from_pressure()
temp = (htemp + ptemp) / 2
print(temp)
```

Click the Run icon, and you'll see a number printed to the Python console (**Figure 7-23**). This time, it's based on readings from both sensors, which you've added together and divided by two – the number of readings – to get an average of both. If you're using the emulator, all three methods – humidity, pressure, and average – will show the same number.

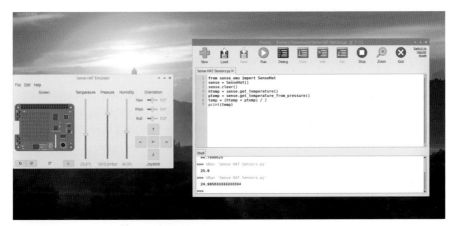

▲ **Figure 7-23:** A temperature based on the readings from both sensors

CHALLENGE: SCROLL & LOOP

Can you change your program to take a reading from each of the sensors in turn, then scroll them across the LED matrix rather than printing them to the shell? Can you make your program loop, so it's constantly printing the current environmental conditions?

Inertial sensing

The gyroscopic sensor, accelerometer, and magnetometer combine to form what is known as an *inertial measurement unit (IMU)*. While, technically speaking, these sensors take measurements from the surrounding environment just like the environmental sensors – the magnetometer, for example, measures magnetic field strength – they're usually used for data about the movement of the Sense HAT itself. The IMU is the sum of multiple sensors; some programming languages allow you to take readings from each sensor independently, while others will only give you a combined reading.

Before you can make sense of the IMU, though, you need to understand how things move. The Sense HAT, and your Raspberry Pi it's attached to, can move along three spatial axes: side-to-side on the X axis; forwards and backwards on the Y axis; and up and down on the Z axis (**Figure 7-24**). It can also rotate along these three same axes, but their names change: rotating on the X axis is called *roll*, rotating on the Y axis is called *pitch*, and rotating on the Z axis is called *yaw*. When you rotate the Sense HAT along its short axis, you're adjusting its pitch; rotate along its long axis and that's roll; spin it around while keeping it flat on the table and you're adjusting its yaw. Think of them like an aeroplane: when it's taking off, it increases its pitch to climb; when it's doing a victory roll, that's literally it spinning along its roll axis; when it's using its rudder to turn like a car would, without rolling, that's yaw.

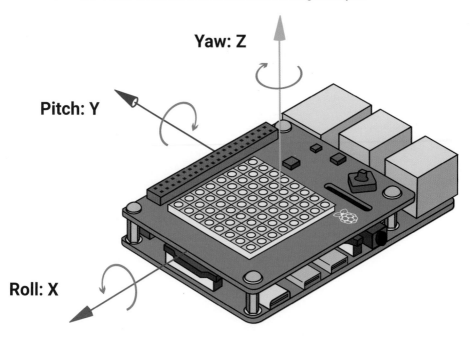

▲ **Figure 7-24:** The spatial axes of the Sense HAT's IMU

Inertial sensing in Scratch

Start a new program in Scratch and load the Raspberry Pi Sense HAT extension, if it's not already loaded. Start your program in the same way as before: drag a `when ⚑ clicked` Events block onto your code area, then drag a `clear display` block underneath it followed by dragging and editing a `set background to black` and a `set colour to white` block.

Next, drag a `forever` block to the bottom of your existing blocks and fill it with a `say Hello!` block. To show a reading for each of the three axes of the IMU – pitch, roll, and yaw – you'll need to add `join` Operator blocks plus the corresponding Sense HAT blocks. Remember to include spaces and commas, so that the output is easy to read.

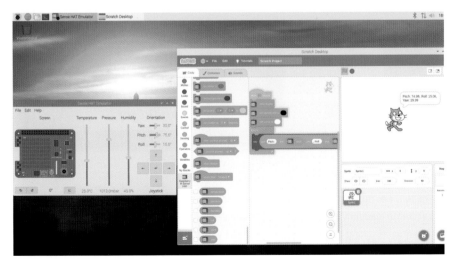

Click the green flag to run your program, and try moving the Sense HAT and Raspberry Pi around – being careful not to dislodge any cables! As you tilt the Sense HAT through its three axes, you'll see the pitch, roll, and yaw values change accordingly (**Figure 7-25**).

▲ **Figure 7-25:** Displaying the pitch, roll, and yaw values

Inertial sensing in Python

Start a new program in Thonny and save it as **Sense HAT Movement**. Fill in the usual starting lines, remembering to use **sense_emu** if you're using the Sense HAT emulator.

```
from sense_hat import SenseHat
sense = SenseHat()
sense.clear()
```

To use information from the IMU to work out the current orientation of the Sense HAT on its three axes, type the following:

```
orientation = sense.get_orientation()
pitch = orientation["pitch"]
roll = orientation["roll"]
yaw = orientation["yaw"]
print("pitch {0} roll {1} yaw {2}".format(pitch, roll, yaw))
```

Click Run and you'll see readings for the Sense HAT's orientation split across the three axes (**Figure 7-26**). Try rotating the Sense HAT and clicking Run again; you should see the numbers change to reflect its new orientation.

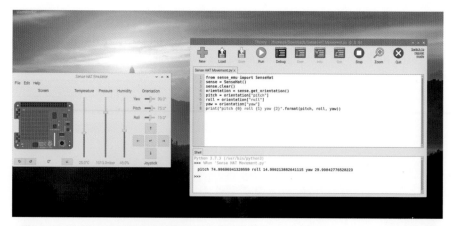

▲ **Figure 7-26:** Showing the Sense HAT's pitch, roll, and yaw values

The IMU can do more than measure orientation, though: it can also detect movement. To get accurate readings for movement, the IMU needs to be read frequently in a loop: unlike for orientation, taking a single reading won't get you any useful information when it comes to detecting movement. Delete everything after **sense.clear()** then type the following code:

```
while True:
    acceleration = sense.get_accelerometer_raw()
    x = acceleration["x"]
    y = acceleration["y"]
    z = acceleration["z"]
```

You now have variables containing the current accelerometer readings for the three spatial axes: X, or left and right; Y, or forwards and backwards; and Z, or up or down. The numbers from the accelerometer sensor can be difficult to read, so type the following to make them easier to understand by rounding them to the nearest whole number:

```
x = round(x)
y = round(y)
z = round(z)
```

Finally, print the three values by typing the following line:

```
print("x={0}, y={1}, z={2}".format(x, y, z))
```

Click Run, and you'll see values from the accelerometer printed to the Python shell area (**Figure 7-27**). Unlike your previous program, these will print continuously; to stop them printing, click the red stop button to stop the program.

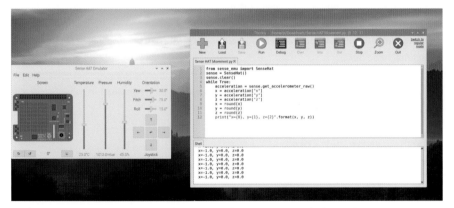

▲ **Figure 7-27:** Accelerometer readings rounded to the nearest whole number

You may have noticed that the accelerometer is telling you that one of the axes – the Z axis, if your Raspberry Pi is flat on the table – has an acceleration value of 1.0 gravities (1G), yet the Sense HAT isn't moving. That's because it's detecting the Earth's gravitational pull – the force that is pulling the Sense HAT down towards the centre of the Earth, and the reason why if you knock something off your desk it'll fall to the floor.

With your program running, try carefully picking the Sense HAT and Raspberry Pi up and rotating them around – but make sure not to dislodge any of its cables! With Raspberry Pi's network and USB ports pointing to the floor, you'll see the values change so the Z axis reads 0G and the X axis now reads 1G; turn it again so the HDMI and power ports are pointing to the floor and now it's the Y axis that reads 1G. If you do the opposite and have the HDMI port pointing to the ceiling, you'll see -1G on the Y axis instead.

Using the knowledge that the Earth's gravity is roughly around 1G, and your knowledge of the spatial axes, you can use readings from the accelerometer to figure out which way is down – and, likewise, which way is up. You can also use it to detect movement: try carefully shaking the Sense HAT and Raspberry Pi, and watch the numbers as you do: the harder you shake, the greater the acceleration.

When you're using **sense.get_accelerometer_raw()**, you're telling the Sense HAT to turn off the other two sensors in the IMU – the gyroscopic sensor and the magnetometer – and return data purely from the accelerometer. Naturally, you can do the same thing with the other sensors too.

Find the line **acceleration = sense.get_accelerometer_raw()** and change it to:

```
orientation = sense.get_gyroscope_raw()
```

Change the word **acceleration** on all three lines below it to **orientation**. Click Run, and you'll see the orientation of the Sense HAT for all three axes, rounded to the nearest whole number. Unlike the last time you checked orientation, though, this time the data is coming purely from the gyroscope without using the accelerometer or magnetometer. This can be useful if you want to know the orientation of a moving Sense HAT on the back of a robot, for example, without the movement confusing matters, or if you're using the Sense HAT near a strong magnetic field

Stop your program by clicking on the red stop button. To use the magnetometer, delete everything from your program except for the first four lines, then type the following below the **while True** line:

```
north = sense.get_compass()
print(north)
```

Run your program and you'll see the direction of magnetic north printed repeatedly to the Python shell area. Carefully rotate the Sense HAT and you'll see the heading change as the Sense HAT's orientation relative to north shifts: you've built a compass! If you have a magnet – a fridge magnet will do – try moving it around the Sense HAT to see what that does to the magnetometer's readings.

CHALLENGE: AUTO-ROTATE

Using what you've learned about the LED matrix and the inertial measurement unit's sensors, can you write a program that rotates an image depending on the position of the Sense HAT?

Joystick control

The Sense HAT's joystick, found in the bottom-right corner, may be small, but it's surprisingly powerful: as well as being able to recognise inputs in four directions – up, down, left, and right – it also has a fifth input, accessed by pushing it down from above like a push-button switch.

WARNING!

The Sense HAT joystick should only be used if you've fitted the spacers as described at the start of this chapter. Without the spacers, pushing down on the joystick can flex the Sense HAT board and damage both the Sense HAT and Raspberry Pi's GPIO header.

Joystick control in Scratch

Start a new program in Scratch with the Raspberry Pi Sense HAT extension loaded. As before, drag a `when ⚑ clicked` Events block onto your script area, then drag a `clear display` block underneath it followed by dragging and editing a `set background to black` and a `set colour to white` block.

In Scratch, the Sense HAT's joystick maps to the cursor keys on the keyboard: pushing the joystick up is equivalent to pressing the up arrow key, pushing it down is the same as pushing the down arrow key, pushing it left the same as the left arrow key, and pushing it right the same as the right arrow key; pushing the joystick inwards like a push-button switch, meanwhile, is equivalent to pressing the **ENTER** key.

WARNING!

Joystick control is only available on the physical Sense HAT. When using the Sense HAT Emulator, use the corresponding keys on your keyboard to simulate joystick presses instead.

Drag a `when joystick pushed up` block onto your code area. Then, to give it something to do, drag a `say Hello! for 2 seconds` block under it.

Push the joystick upwards and you'll see the Scratch cat say a cheery "Hello!"

Next, edit the `say Hello! for 2 seconds` block into a `say Joystick Up! for 2 seconds` block, and continue to add Events and Looks blocks until you have something for each of the five ways the joystick can be pressed.

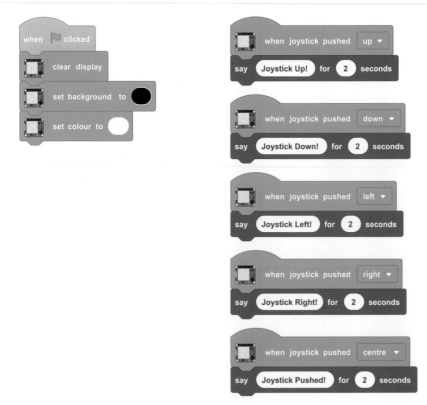

Try pushing the joystick in various directions to see your messages appear!

FINAL CHALLENGE

Can you use the Sense HAT's joystick to control a Scratch sprite on the stage area? Can you make it so if the sprite collects another sprite, representing an object, the Sense HAT's LEDs display a cheery message?

Joystick control in Python

Start a new program in Thonny and save it as Sense HAT Joystick. Begin with the usual three lines that set up the Sense HAT and clear the LED matrix:

```
from sense_hat import SenseHat
sense = SenseHat()
sense.clear()
```

Next, set up an infinite loop:

```
while True:
```

Then tell Python to listen for inputs from the Sense HAT joystick with the following line, which Thonny will automatically indent for you:

```
    for event in sense.stick.get_events():
```

Finally, add the following line – which, again Thonny will indent for you – to actually do something when a joystick press is detected:

```
        print(event.direction, event.action)
```

Click Run, and try pushing the joystick in various directions. You'll see the direction you've chosen printed to the Python shell area: up, down, left, right, and middle for when you've pushed the joystick down like a push-button switch.

You'll also see that you're given two events each time you push the joystick once: one event, **pressed**, for when you first push a direction; the other event, **released**, for when the joystick returns to centre. You can use this in your programs: think of a character in a game, which could be made to start moving when the joystick is pressed in a direction then stop as soon as it's released.

You can also use the joystick to trigger functions, rather than being limited to using a for loop. Delete everything below **sense.clear()**, and type the following:

```python
def red():
    sense.clear(255, 0, 0)

def blue():
    sense.clear(0, 0, 255)

def green():
    sense.clear(0, 255, 0)

def yellow():
    sense.clear(255, 255, 0)
```

These functions change the whole Sense HAT LED matrix to a single colour: red, blue, green, or yellow – which is going to make seeing that your program works extremely easy! To actually trigger them, you need to tell Python which function goes with which joystick input. Type the following lines:

```python
sense.stick.direction_up = red
sense.stick.direction_down = blue
sense.stick.direction_left = green
sense.stick.direction_right = yellow
sense.stick.direction_middle = sense.clear
```

Finally, the program needs an infinite loop – known as the *main* loop – in order to keep running, and therefore keep watching for joystick inputs, rather than just running through the code you've written once and quitting. Type the following two lines:

```python
while True:
    pass
```

Click Run, and try moving the joystick: you'll see the LEDs light up in glorious colour! To turn the LEDs off, push the joystick like a push-button: the **middle** direction is set to use the **sense.clear()** function to turn them all off. Congratulations: you can capture input from the joystick!

FINAL CHALLENGE

Can you use what you've learned to draw an image to the screen, then have it rotated in whatever direction the joystick is pushed? Can you make the middle input switch between more than one picture?

Scratch project: Sense HAT Sparkler

Now you know your way around the Sense HAT, it's time to put everything you've learned together to build a heat-sensitive sparkler – a device which is at its happiest when it's cold and which gradually slows down the hotter it gets.

Start a new Scratch project and add the Raspberry Pi Sense HAT extension, if not already loaded. As always, begin with four blocks: `when clicked`, `clear display`, `set background to black`, and `set colour to white`, remembering you'll have to change the colours from their default settings.

Start by creating a simple, but artistic, sparkler. Drag a `forever` block onto the code area, then fill it with a `set pixel x 0 y 0 to colour` block. Rather than using set numbers, fill in each of the x, y, and colour sections of that block with a `pick random 1 to 10` Operators block.

The values 1 to 10 aren't very useful here, so you need to do some editing. The first two numbers in the `set pixel` block are the X and Y coordinates of the pixel on the LED matrix, which means they should be number between 0 and 7 – so change the first two blocks to read `pick random 0 to 7`. The next section is the colour the pixel should be set to. When you're using the colour selector, the colour you choose is shown directly in the script area; internally, though, the colours are represented by a number, and you can use the number directly. Edit the last pick random block to read `pick random 0 to 16777215`.

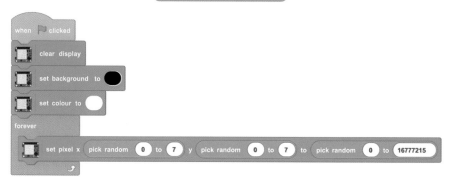

Click the green flag and you'll see the LEDs on the Sense HAT begin to light up in random colours (**Figure 7-28**, overleaf). Congratulations: you've made an electronic sparkler!

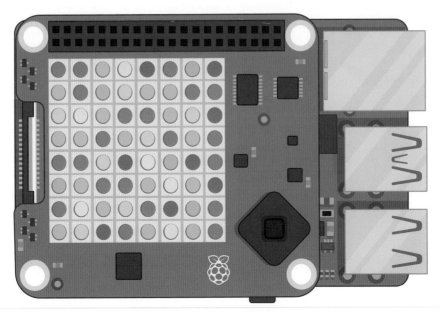

▲ **Figure 7-28:** Lighting the pixels in random colours

The sparkler isn't very interactive. To change that, start by dragging a `wait 1 seconds` block so it's under the `set pixel` block but within the `forever` block. Drag a `◯ / ◯` Operators block over the 1, then type 10 in its second space. Finally, drag a `temperature` block over the first space in the divide Operator block.

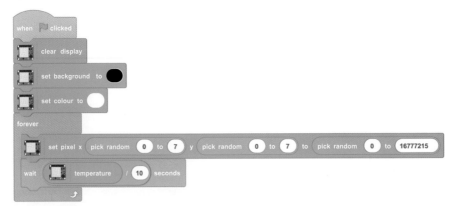

Click the green flag and you'll notice – unless you live somewhere very cold – that the sparkler is considerably slower than before. That's because you've created a temperature-dependent delay: the program now waits *the current temperature divided by 10* number of seconds before each loop. If the temperature in your room is 20°C, the program will wait 2 seconds before looping; if the temperature is 10°C, it'll wait 1 second; if it's under 10°C, it'll wait less than a second.

If your Sense HAT is reading a negative temperature – below 0°C, the freezing point of water – it'll try to wait less than 0 seconds; because that's impossible – without inventing time travel, anyway – you'll see the same effect as though it was waiting 0 seconds. Congratulations: you can now look at integrating the Sense HAT's various features into programs of your own!

Python project: Sense HAT Tricorder

Now you know your way around the Sense HAT, it's time to put everything you've learned together to build a tricorder – a device immediately familiar to fans of a certain science-fiction franchise as being able to report on various sensors built into it.

Start a new project in Thonny and save it as **Tricorder**, then start with the traditional lines you need to make a Sense HAT program:

```python
from sense_hat import SenseHat
sense = SenseHat()
sense.clear()
```

Next, you need to start defining functions for each of the Sense HAT's various sensors. Start with the inertial measurement unit by typing:

```python
def orientation():
    orientation = sense.get_orientation()
    pitch = orientation["pitch"]
    roll = orientation["roll"]
    yaw = orientation["yaw"]
```

Because you're going to be scrolling the results from the sensor across the LEDs, it makes sense to round them so that you're not waiting for dozens of decimal places. Rather than whole numbers, though, round them to one decimal place by typing the following:

```python
    pitch = round(pitch, 1)
    roll = round(roll, 1)
    yaw = round(yaw, 1)
```

Finally, you need to tell Python to scroll the results to the LEDs, so the tricorder works as a hand-held device without needing to be connected to a monitor or TV:

```python
    sense.show_message("Pitch {0}, Roll {1}, Yaw {2}".
format(pitch, roll, yaw))
```

Now that you have a full function for reading and displaying the orientation from the IMU, you need to create similar functions for each of the other sensors. Start with the temperature sensor.

```python
def temperature():
    temp = sense.get_temperature()
    temp = round(temp, 1)
    sense.show_message("Temperature: %s degrees Celsius" % temp)
```

Look carefully at the line which prints the result to the LEDs: the **%s** is known as a placeholder, and gets replaced with the content of the variable **temp**. Using this, you can format the output nicely with a label, 'Temperature:', and a unit of measurement, 'degrees Celsius,' which makes your program a lot more friendly.

Next, define a function for the humidity sensor:

```python
def humidity():
    humidity = sense.get_humidity()
    humidity = round(humidity, 1)
    sense.show_message("Humidity: %s percent" % humidity)
```

Then the pressure sensor:

```python
def pressure():
    pressure = sense.get_pressure()
    pressure = round(pressure, 1)
    sense.show_message("Pressure: %s millibars" % pressure)
```

And finally the compass reading from the magnetometer:

```python
def compass():
    for i in range(0, 10):
        north = sense.get_compass()
    north = round(north, 1)
    sense.show_message("North: %s degrees" % north)
```

The short **for** loop in this function takes ten readings from the magnetometer to ensure that it has enough data to give you an accurate result. If you find that the reported value keeps shifting, try extending it to 20, 30, or even 100 loops to improve the accuracy further.

Your program now has five functions, each of which takes a reading from one of the Sense HAT's sensors and scrolls them across the LEDs. It needs a way to choose which sensor you want to use, though, and the joystick is perfect for that.

Type the following:

```python
sense.stick.direction_up = orientation
sense.stick.direction_right = temperature
```

```
sense.stick.direction_down = compass
sense.stick.direction_left = humidity
sense.stick.direction_middle = pressure
```

These lines assign a sensor to each of the five possible directions on the joystick: up reads from the orientation sensor; down reads from the magnetometer; left reads from the humidity sensor; right from the temperature sensor; and pressing the stick in the middle reads from the pressure sensor.

Finally, you need a main loop so the program will keep listening out for joystick presses and not just immediately quit. At the very bottom of your program, type the following:

```
while True:
    pass
```

Click Run, and try moving the joystick to take a reading from one of the sensors (**Figure 7-29**). When it has finished scrolling the result, press a different direction. Congratulations: you've built a hand-held tricorder that would make the Federation of Planets proud!

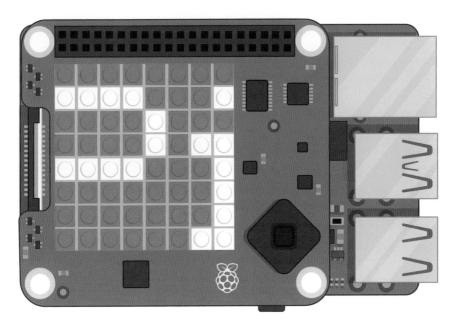

▲ **Figure 7-29:** Each reading scrolls across the display

For more Sense HAT projects, follow the links in **Appendix D, Further reading**.

Chapter 8
Raspberry Pi Camera Module

Connecting a Raspberry Pi Camera Module to Raspberry Pi enables you to take high-resolution photos and shoot videos, and create amazing computer vision projects

I f you've ever wanted to build something that can see – known in the robotics field as *computer vision* – then Raspberry Pi's optional Camera Module is a great starting place. A small square circuit board with a thin ribbon cable, the Camera Module connects to the Camera Serial Interface (CSI) port on your Raspberry Pi and provides high-resolution still images and moving video signals which can be used as is or integrated into your own programs.

CAMERA TYPES!

There are two versions of the Raspberry Pi Camera Module available: the normal version and the 'NoIR' version. You can easily tell the difference: the normal version has a green circuit board, while the NoIR version has a black circuit board. If you want to take normal pictures and video in well-lit environments, you should always use the normal version for best image quality. The NoIR version – so called because it has no infrared, or IR, filter – is designed for use with infrared light sources to take pictures and video in total darkness. If you're building a nest box, security camera, or other project involving night vision, you want the NoIR version – but remember to buy an infrared light source at the same time!

At the time of writing, the current version of the Raspberry Pi Camera Module, known as the 'v2' module or 'Version 2.1', is based on a high-quality Sony IMX219 image sensor – the same type of sensor you might find on the back of your smartphone or tablet. This is an *8 megapixel sensor*, which means it can take pictures with up to 8 million pixels in them. It does this by capturing images up to 3280 pixels wide by 2464 tall: multiply those two numbers together and you get a total of just over 8 million individual pixels!

As well as still images, the Camera Module can capture video footage at Full HD resolution – the same resolution as most TVs – at a rate of 30 frames per second (30 fps). For smoother motion or even to create a slow-motion effect, the camera can be set to capture at a higher frame rate by lowering the resolution: 60fps for 720p video footage, and up to 90 fps for 480p – or 'VGA' resolution – footage.

Installing the Camera Module

Like any hardware add-on, the Camera Module should only be connected to or disconnected from Raspberry Pi when the power is off and the power cable unplugged. If your Raspberry Pi is on, choose Shutdown from the raspberry menu, wait for it to power off, and unplug it.

Unpack your Camera Module: you'll find a small circuit board, which is the Camera Module itself, and a flat ribbon cable. In most cases, the ribbon cable will already be connected to the Camera Module; if it isn't, turn your Module upside-down so the camera lens is on the bottom and look for a flat plastic connector. Carefully hook your fingernails around the sticking-out edges and pull outwards until the connector pulls part-way out. Slide the ribbon cable, with the silver edges downwards and the blue plastic facing upwards, under the flap you just pulled out, then push the flap gently back into place with a click (**Figure 8-1** overleaf); it doesn't matter which end of the cable you use. If the cable is installed properly, it will be straight and won't come out if you give it a gentle tug; if not, pull the flap out and try again.

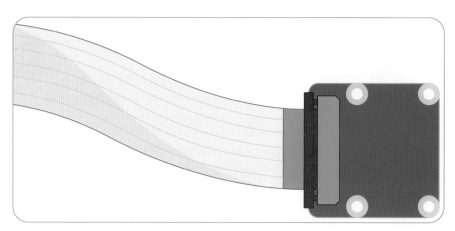

▲ **Figure 8-1:** Connecting the ribbon cable to the Camera Module

Install the other end of the cable the same way. Find the Camera (or CSI) port on Raspberry Pi and pull the flap gently upwards. If your Raspberry Pi is installed in a case, you might find it easier to remove it first. With Raspberry Pi positioned so the HDMI port is facing you, slide the ribbon cable in so the silver edges are to your left and the blue plastic to your right (**Figure 8-2**), then gently push the flap back into place. If the cable is installed properly, it'll be straight and won't come out if you give it a gentle tug; if not, pull the flap out and try again.

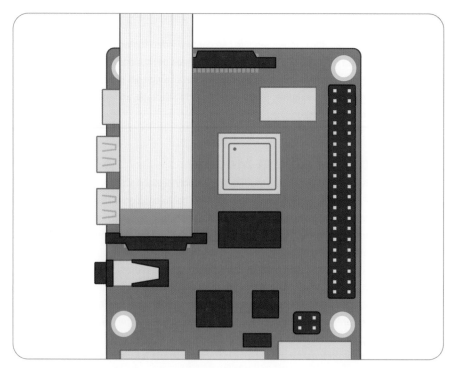

▲ **Figure 8-2:** Connecting the ribbon cable to the Camera/CSI port on Raspberry Pi

The Camera Module comes with a small piece of blue plastic covering the lens, in order to protect it from scratches during manufacturing, shipping, and installation. Find the small flap of plastic and pull it gently off the lens to get the camera ready for use.

ADJUSTING FOCUS

The Raspberry Pi Camera Module is usually supplied with a small plastic wheel. This is designed for adjusting the focus of the lens. While the factory-set focus is usually perfect, if you're using your camera for very close-up work you can slide the wheel over the lens and gently twist it to adjust the focus manually.

Connect the power supply back to Raspberry Pi and let it load Raspbian. Before you can use the camera, you'll need to tell Raspberry Pi it has one connected: click the raspberry icon to load the menu, choose the Preferences category, and click Raspberry Pi Configuration. When the tool has loaded, click the Interfaces tab, find the Camera entry in the list, and click on the round radio button to the left of 'Enabled' to switch it on (**Figure 8-3**). Click OK, and the tool will prompt you to reboot your Raspberry Pi. Do so and your camera will be ready to use!

Raspberry Pi Configuration				
System	Display	Interfaces	Performance	Localisation
Camera:	● Enabled	○ Disabled		
SSH:	● Enabled	○ Disabled		
VNC:	○ Enabled	● Disabled		
SPI:	○ Enabled	● Disabled		
I2C:	○ Enabled	● Disabled		
Serial Port:	○ Enabled	● Disabled		
Serial Console:	● Enabled	○ Disabled		
1-Wire:	○ Enabled	● Disabled		
Remote GPIO:	○ Enabled	● Disabled		
			Cancel	OK

▲ **Figure 8-3:** You need to enable the camera in Raspberry Pi Configuration

Testing the Camera Module

To confirm that your Camera Module is properly installed, and that you've enabled the interface in the Raspberry Pi Configuration Tool, you can use the **raspistill** tool. This, along with **raspivid** for videos, is designed to capture images from the camera using Raspberry Pi's *command-line interface (CLI)*.

Unlike the programs you've been using so far, you won't find raspistill in the menu. Instead, click on the raspberry icon to load the menu, choose the Accessories category, and click on Terminal. A black window with green and blue writing in it will appear (**Figure 8-4**): this is the *terminal*, which allows you to access the command-line interface.

▲ **Figure 8-4:** Open a Terminal window to enter commands

To test the camera, type the following into the Terminal:

```
raspistill -o test.jpg
```

As soon as you hit **ENTER**, you'll see a large picture of what the camera sees appear on-screen (**Figure 8-5**). This is called the *live preview* and, unless you tell raspistill otherwise, it will last for 5 seconds. After those 5 seconds are up, the camera will capture a single still picture and save it in your home folder under the name **test.jpg**. If you want to capture another, type the same command again – but make sure to change the output file name, after the **-o**, or you'll save over the top of your first picture!

▲ **Figure 8-5:** The live preview from the camera

If the live preview was upside-down, you'll need to tell raspistill that the camera is rotated. The Camera Module is designed to have the ribbon cable coming out of the bottom edge; if it's coming out of the sides or the top, as with some third-party camera mount accessories, you can rotate the image by 90, 180, or 270 degrees using the **-rot** switch. For a camera mounted with the cable coming out of the top, simply use the following command:

```
raspistill -rot 180 -o test.jpg
```

If the ribbon cable is coming out of the right-hand edge, use a rotation value of 90 degrees; if it's coming out of the left-hand edge, use 270 degrees. If your original capture was at the wrong angle, try another using the **-rot** switch to correct it.

To see your picture, open the File Manager from the Accessories category of the raspberry menu: the image you've taken, called **test.jpg**, will be in your **home/pi** folder. Find it in the list of files, then double-click it to load it in an image viewer (**Figure 8-6**). You can also attach the image to emails, upload it to websites via the browser, or drag it to an external storage device.

▲ **Figure 8-6:** Opening the captured image

Introducing picamera

The most flexible way to control the Camera Module is using Python, via the handy picamera library. This gives you full control over the Camera Module's preview, picture, and video capture abilities, and allows you to integrate them into your own programs – even combining them with programs which use the GPIO module through the GPIO Zero library!

PYTHON PROGRAMMING

The projects in this chapter assume experience with the Python programming language, Thonny IDE, and Raspberry Pi's GPIO pins. If you haven't done so already, please work through the projects in **Chapter 5, Programming with Python**, and **Chapter 6, Physical computing with Scratch and Python**, first!

Close the Terminal, if it's still open, by clicking on the X at the top-right of the window, then load Thonny from the Programming category of the raspberry menu. Save your new project as **Camera**, then start importing the libraries your program needs by typing the following into the script area:

```
from picamera import PiCamera
from time import sleep
camera = PiCamera()
```

The last line allows you to control the Camera Module using the **camera** function. To start, type the following:

```
camera.start_preview()
sleep(10)
camera.stop_preview()
```

Click Run, and your desktop will disappear; in its place, you'll see a full-screen preview of whatever the camera can see (**Figure 8-7**). Try moving it around, or waving your hand in front of the lens, and you'll see the picture on screen change to match. After 10 seconds the preview will close and your program will finish – but, unlike the preview from raspistill, no picture will be saved afterwards.

▲ **Figure 8-7:** A full-screen live preview of the camera view

If your preview was the wrong way up, you can rotate the image to get it the right way up again. Just under the line **camera = PiCamera()**, type:

```
camera.rotation = 180
```

If the preview was upside-down, that line will get things looking right again. As with raspistill, **camera.rotation** lets you rotate the image by 90, 180, or 270 degrees, depending on whether the cable is coming out of the right, top, or left side of the Camera Module. Remember to use **camera.rotation** at the start of any program you write, to avoid capturing images or video that are the wrong way up!

Capturing still pictures

To capture a picture, rather than just show a live preview, your program needs to be changed. Start by reducing the delay for the preview: find the **sleep(10)** line, and change it to read:

```
sleep(5)
```

Directly under that line, add the following:

```
camera.capture('/home/pi/Desktop/image.jpg')
```

TIME TO ADJUST

When the camera is in preview mode, it analyses the video to see if it needs to adjust its settings to get the best quality. You'll see this if you're in a very dark or very light environment, with the preview at first being impossible to see, then quickly getting clearer. To give the camera time to adjust, always add at least a 2-second preview period to your program before capturing an image.

The **camera.capture** function tells Python to save a still image, and it needs to know not only what the image should be called but in what folder it should be saved. In this example, you're saving it to the desktop – find it by looking just below the Wastebasket. If the Thonny window is in the way, just click and drag on the title bar to move it. Double-click on the file to see the image you captured (**Figure 8-8**). Congratulations: you've programmed a camera!

▲ **Figure 8-8:** Opening the captured image

Capturing moving video

As well as taking still images, you can capture video. Delete everything between the lines **camera.start_preview()** and **camera.stop_preview()**, then type the following under **camera.start_preview()**:

```
camera.start_recording('/home/pi/Desktop/video.h264')
sleep(10)
camera.stop_recording()
```

The camera preview will appear, as before, but this time it will also be recorded to a file on the desktop. Wait for the 10 seconds you've told Python to sleep – perhaps do a little dance in front of the camera to make the video interesting – then, when the preview has closed, you'll find your video file on the desktop.

To play the video, simply double-click on the **video.h264** file on your desktop. The video will start playing – and if you did a dance, you'll see it played back to you! After the video has finished, the player software will quit with a friendly message in the Terminal. Congratulations: you can now capture video using your Raspberry Pi Camera Module!

Push-button stop-motion animation

Using what you've learned in this chapter, and your knowledge of how to connect hardware to Raspberry Pi's GPIO header from **Chapter 6**, **Physical Computing**, it's time to build something special: your very own stop-motion animation studio.

Stop-motion animation is the process of taking lots of pictures of still objects, like model cars or action figures, and moving the objects slightly between each picture. Although the objects never move in any of the pictures, if you show them one after another quickly enough it'll look like they're moving as quickly or as slowly as you like!

For this project, you'll need a push-button switch, a breadboard, a male-to-male (M2M) jumper wire, and a pair of male-to-female (M2F) jumper wires. If you don't have a breadboard you can connect the switch using female-to-female (F2F) cables instead, but it will be more difficult to press. If you need reminding about any of these components, turn to **Chapter 6, Physical computing with Scratch and Python**. You'll also need objects to animate: these can be anything from a blob of clay to a toy car or an action figure.

Start by creating the circuit: add the push-button to the breadboard, then connect the ground rail of the breadboard to a ground pin on Raspberry Pi (marked GND on **Figure 8-9** overleaf) with a male-to-female jumper wire. Use a male-to-male jumper wire to connect one leg of the switch to the ground rail on the breadboard, then a male-to-female jumper wire to connect the other leg of the switch to GPIO pin 2 (marked GP2 on **Figure 8-9**).

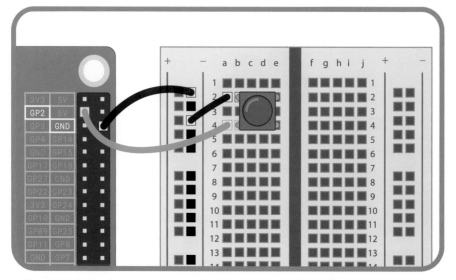

▲ **Figure 8-9:** Wiring diagram for connecting a push-button to the GPIO pins

Create a new project in Thonny and save it as **Stop Motion**. Start by importing and setting up the libraries you need for using the camera and the GPIO port:

```
from picamera import PiCamera
from gpiozero import Button
camera = PiCamera()
button = Button(2)
```

Next, type the following:

```
camera.start_preview()
button.wait_for_press()
camera.capture('/home/pi/Desktop/image.jpg')
camera.stop_preview()
```

Click Run and you'll see a preview of whatever your Camera Module is pointing at. The preview will stay on screen until you press the push-button switch: press it now, and the preview will close after your program saves a picture to the desktop. Find the picture, called **image.jpg**, and double-click to open it and confirm the program is working.

Stop-motion animation involves creating lots of still images, to give the impression of movement when they're all put together. Having all these individual pictures on your desktop would make a mess, so you need a folder to store them all. Right-click anywhere on the desktop that doesn't already have a file or an icon, then choose Create New and Folder (**Figure 8-10**). Call the folder **animation**, all in lower-case letters, then click the OK button.

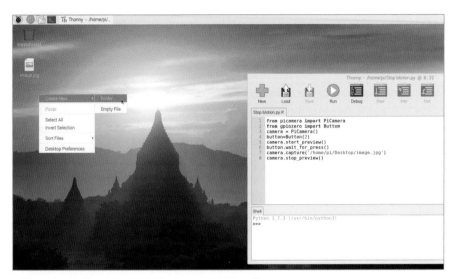

▲ **Figure 8-10:** Create a new folder for your captured images

Having to restart your program every time you capture a picture for your animation isn't very good, so you need to change it to run in a loop. Unlike the previous loops you've created, though, this one needs a way to close gracefully – otherwise, if you stop the program while the camera preview is showing, you won't be able to see the desktop any more! To do this, you need to use two special instructions: **try** and **except**.

Start by deleting everything after `camera.start_preview(),` then typing:

```
frame = 1
```

This creates a new variable, **frame**, which your program will use to store the current frame number. You'll use this shortly to ensure that you're saving a new file every time; without it, you'll just be saving over the top of your first image every time you press the button!

Next, set up your loop by typing:

```
while True:
    try:
```

The new instruction **try** tells Python to run whatever code is inside – which is going to be the code for capturing images. Type:

```
button.wait_for_press()
camera.capture('/home/pi/Desktop/animation/frame%03d.jpg' % frame)
frame += 1
```

There are a couple of clever tricks in these three lines of code. The first is in the capture file name: using **%03d** tells Python to take a number and add as many zeroes to the front as it needs to make it three digits long. Thus '1' becomes '001', '2' becomes '002', and '10' becomes '010'. You need this in your program to keep your files in the correct order and to make sure you're not writing over a file you've already saved.

The **% frame** at the end of that line tells Python to use the number of the frame variable in the file name. To make sure each file is unique, the last line – **frame += 1** – increments the frame variable by 1. The first time you press the button, **frame** will be increased from 1 to 2; the next time, from 2 to 3; and so on.

At the moment, though, your code won't exit cleanly when you're finished taking pictures. To make that happen, you need an **except** for your **try**. Type the following, remembering to remove one level of indentation on the first line so Python knows it's not part of the **try** section:

```
except KeyboardInterrupt:
    camera.stop_preview()
    break
```

Your finished program will look like this:

```
from picamera import PiCamera
from time import sleep
from gpiozero import Button
camera = PiCamera()
button = Button(2)
camera.start_preview()
frame = 1
while True:
    try:
        button.wait_for_press()
        camera.capture('/home/pi/Desktop/animation/frame%03d.jpg'
% frame)
        frame += 1
    except KeyboardInterrupt:
        camera.stop_preview()
        break
```

Try clicking Run, but instead of pressing the button, press the **CTRL** and **C** keys on the keyboard. You don't need to press both keys at the same time: just hold down **CTRL**, press and release **C**, then release **CTRL**. These two keys act as an interrupt, telling Python to stop what it's doing. Without the **except KeyboardInterrupt:** line, Python would immediately quit and leave the camera preview blocking your screen; with that line in place, though, Python runs whatever code is inside – in this case, code telling it to stop the camera preview and exit cleanly.

Now you're ready to start capturing your stop-motion animation! Position the Camera Module where it can see the objects you're going to animate, and make sure it won't move – if the camera moves, it spoils the effect. Place your objects in their starting positions, then click Run to launch your program. Check everything looks good in the preview, and press the push-button to capture your first frame.

Move the objects slightly – the less you move them between frames, the smoother the finished animation will be – and press the push-button again to capture another frame. Keep doing this until your animation is finished: the more frames you capture, the longer your animation will be.

When you've finished, press **CTRL+C** to close your program, then double-click on the **animation** folder on the desktop to see the pictures you've captured (**Figure 8-11**). Double-click on any picture to open it and see it in more detail!

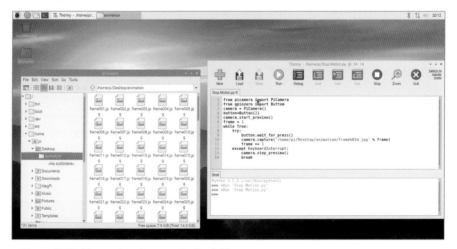

▲ **Figure 8-11:** The captured images in the folder

At the moment, though, all you have is a folder full of still images. To create an animation, you need to turn them into a video. To do so, click on the raspberry icon to load the menu, choose Accessories, and click on Terminal. This opens a *command-line interface*, discussed in more detail in **Appendix C**, which allows you to type commands to Raspberry Pi. When the Terminal loads, start by changing into the folder you made by typing:

```
cd Desktop/animation
```

It's important that the 'D' of 'Desktop' is in upper-case; Raspbian is what is known as case-sensitive, which means if you don't type a command or folder name exactly as it was originally written, it won't work! Once you've changed folders, type the following:

```
avconv -r 1 -i frame%03d.jpg -r 10 animation.h264
```

This uses a program called **avconv** to take the still images in the folder and convert them into a video called **animation.h264**. Depending on how many stills you took, this process can take a few minutes; you'll know it's finished when you see the Terminal prompt reappear.

To play the video, find the file **animation.h264** in your **animation** folder and double-click it to open it. Alternatively, you can play it back from the Terminal by typing the following:

```
omxplayer animation.h264
```

Once the video has loaded, you'll see your stop-motion animation come to life. Congratulations: you've turned your Raspberry Pi into a powerful animation studio!

If your animation is moving too quickly or too slowly, change the **-r 10** part of the **avconv** command to a lower or higher number: this is the frame rate, or how many still images there are in one second of video. A lower number will make your animation run more slowly, but look less smooth; a higher number looks smoother, but will make the animation run more quickly.

If you want to save your video, be sure to drag and drop it from the desktop to your Videos folder; otherwise, next time you run your program, you'll end up overwriting the file!

Advanced camera settings

If you need more control over the Raspberry Pi Camera Module, you can use the Python picamera library to access various settings. These settings, along with their default values, are detailed below for inclusion in your own programs.

```
camera.awb_mode = 'auto'
```
This sets the automatic white balance mode of the camera, and can be set to any one of the following modes: **off**, **auto**, **sunlight**, **cloudy**, **shade**, **tungsten**, **fluorescent**, **incandescent**, **flash**, or **horizon**. If you find your pictures and videos look a little blue or yellow, try a different mode.

```
camera.brightness = 50
```
This sets the brightness of the camera image, from darkest at 0 to brightest at 100.

```
camera.color_effects = None
```
This changes the colour effect currently in use by the camera. Normally, this setting should be left alone, but if you provide a pair of numbers you can alter the way the camera records colour: try **(128, 128)** to create a black and white image.

`camera.contrast = 0`
This sets the contrast of the image. A higher number will make things look more dramatic and stark; a lower number will make things look more washed out. You can use any number between -100 for minimum contrast and 100 for maximum contrast.

`camera.crop = (0.0, 0.0, 1.0, 1.0)`
This allows you to crop the image, cutting parts off the sides and tops to capture only the part of the image you need. The numbers represent X coordinate, Y coordinate, width, and height, and by default captures the full image. Try reducing the last two numbers – 0.5 and 0.5 is a good starting point – to see what effect this setting has.

`camera.exposure_compensation = 0`
This sets the exposure *compensation* of the camera, allowing you to manually control how much light is captured for each image. Unlike changing the brightness setting, this actually controls the camera itself. Valid values range from -25 for a very dark image to 25 for a very bright image.

`camera.exposure_mode = 'auto'`
This sets the *exposure mode*, or the logic the Camera Module uses to decide how an image should be exposed. Possible modes are: **off**, **auto**, **night**, **backlight**, **spotlight**, **sports**, **snow**, **beach**, **verylong**, **fixedfps**, **antishake**, and **fireworks**.

`camera.framerate = 30`
This sets the number of images captured to create a video per second, or the *frame rate*. A higher frame rate creates a smoother video, but takes up more storage space. Higher frame rates require a lower resolution to be used, which you can set via **camera.resolution**.

`camera.hflip = False`
This flips the camera image across the horizontal, or X, axis when set to **True**.

`camera.image_effect = 'none'`
This applies one of a range of image effects to the video stream, which will be visible in the preview as well as the saved images and videos. Possible effects are: **blur**, **cartoon**, **colorbalance**, **colorpoint**, **colorswap**, **deinterlace1**, **deinterlace2**, **denoise**, **emboss**, **film**, **gpen**, **hatch**, **negative**, **none**, **oilpaint**, **pastel**, **posterise**, **saturation**, **sketch**, **solarize**, **washedout**, and **watercolor**.

`camera.ISO = 0`
This changes the ISO setting of the camera, which affects how sensitive it is to light. By default, the camera adjusts this automatically depending on the available light. You can set the ISO yourself using one of the following values: 100, 200, 320, 400, 500, 640, 800. The higher the ISO, the better the camera will perform in low-light environments but the grainier the image or video it captures.

`camera.meter_mode = 'average'`

This controls how the camera decides on the amount of available light when setting its exposure. The default averages the amount of light available throughout the whole picture; other possible modes are **backlit**, **matrix**, and **spot**.

`camera.resolution = (1920, 1080)`

This sets the resolution of the captured picture or video, represented by two numbers for width and height. Lower resolutions will take up less storage space and allow you to use a higher frame rate; higher resolutions are better quality but take up more storage space.

`camera.rotation = 0`

This controls the rotation of the image, from 0 degrees through 90, 180, and 270 degrees. Use this if you can't position the camera so that the ribbon cable is coming out of the bottom.

`camera.saturation = 0`

This controls the saturation of the image, or how vibrant colours are. Possible values range from -100 to 100.

`camera.sharpness = 0`

This controls the sharpness of the image. Possible values range from -100 to 100.

`camera.shutter_speed = 0`

This controls how quickly the shutter opens and closes when capturing images and videos. You can set the shutter speed manually in microseconds, with longer shutter speeds working better in lower light and faster shutter speeds in brighter light. This should normally be left on its default, automatic, setting.

`camera.vflip = False`

This flips the camera image across the horizontal, or Y, axis when set to **True**.

`camera.video_stabilization = False`

When set to **True**, this turns on video stabilisation. You only need this if the Camera Module is moving while you're recording, such as if it's attached to a robot or being carried, in order to reduce the shakiness of the captured video.

More information on these settings, as well as additional settings not documented here, can be found at **picamera.readthedocs.io**.

Appendix A
Installing NOOBS to a microSD card

The New Out Of the Box Software (NOOBS) is designed to make it as easy as possible to install and set up operating systems on your Raspberry Pi. You can buy microSD cards with NOOBS pre-installed on them from all good Raspberry Pi retailers, or you can use the following instructions to install them to your own microSD card.

> **WARNING!**
>
> If you've purchased a microSD card with NOOBS already pre-installed, you don't need to do anything else other than plug it into your Raspberry Pi. These instructions are for blank microSD cards, or for cards you want to restore back to a factory-fresh condition. Carrying out these instructions on a microSD card with files on it will lose those files, so make sure you've backed things up first!

Downloading NOOBS

To install NOOBS onto a new blank or previously used microSD card, you'll first need to download it from the Raspberry Pi website. On a computer with a microSD card reader, or a full-size SD card reader and a microSD card adapter, open the web browser and type **rpf.io/downloads** into its address bar. From the page that loads, click NOOBS – marked with a raspberry icon – then click 'Download ZIP' under 'NOOBS Offline and network install'.

Products   Blog   Downloads   Community   Help   Forums   Education   Projects   🔍

NOOBS

Beginners should start with NOOBS – New Out Of the Box Software. You can purchase a pre-installed NOOBS SD card from many retailers, such as Pimoroni, Adafruit and The Pi Hut, or download NOOBS below and follow the software setup guide and NOOBS setup guide video in our help pages.

NOOBS is an easy operating system installer which contains Raspbian and LibreELEC. It also provides a selection of alternative operating systems which are then downloaded from the internet and installed.

NOOBS Lite contains the same operating system installer without Raspbian pre-loaded. It provides the same operating system selection menu allowing Raspbian and other images to be downloaded and installed.

NOOBS
Offline and network install

Version: 3.1.1
Release date: 2019-06-24

⬇ Download Torrent   ⬇ Download ZIP

NOOBS Lite
Network install only

Version: 3.1
Release date: 2019-06-24

⬇ Download Torrent   ⬇ Download ZIP

The NOOBS download is quite large, and can take a while to download on a slower internet connection. When the download has finished, plug your microSD card into your PC. It should show up as a single removable drive; if it doesn't, it may need to be *formatted* first.

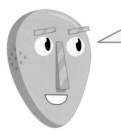

TWO OPTIONS

You may have noticed that there are two NOOBS download options: NOOBS and NOOBS Lite. NOOBS downloads both NOOBS and a copy of the latest Raspbian in a single bundle; NOOBS Lite downloads just NOOBS itself. Most users will want NOOBS; only download NOOBS Lite if you're planning to install an operating system other than Raspbian. Both versions install in the same way, as described in this appendix.

Formatting the microSD

To format a previously used microSD card ready for NOOBS, Windows, and macOS users should download the SD Card Association SD Memory Card Formatter tool from **rpf.io/sdcard**, then double-click to install it; Linux users should use their distribution's disk management tool to delete any existing partitions on the disk, create a single partition, and format it as VFAT, then move onto the next section of this guide.

Insert your microSD card into your card reader, if you haven't done so already, and load the SD Card Formatter tool. Look for your microSD card in the 'Select card' list; if you're reformatting a microSD card that has already been used with a Raspberry Pi, you may find it has more than one entry – just select any one of them. Double-check that you selected the correct drive by looking at the 'Card information' section: it should report the size and type of the microSD card you inserted. If the information is wrong, select a different entry from the 'Select card' list and check again.

When you're absolutely sure you've picked the correct microSD card, and you've backed up any files you want to keep if it's a used card, type 'NOOBS' into the 'Volume label' box, click the Format button, and confirm you want to overwrite the card. The default 'quick format' mode should only take a few seconds to complete, after which you can close the SD Card Formatter.

Installing NOOBS

Installing NOOBS is as simple as drag-and-drop. Start by finding the NOOBS file, which should be in your Downloads folder. This file is known as an *archive*, a single file containing copies of lots of individual files which have been *compressed* to save space and make them quicker and easier to download.

Double-click on the archive to open it, then press **CTRL+A** on your keyboard – ⌘+**A** on macOS – to select all the files in the archive. Click on one of the files with the left mouse button, and drag them to the removable drive representing your microSD card. Let go of the mouse button to drop the files, and wait for them to copy to the microSD; this can take a few minutes.

When the files have successfully copied, eject the microSD card from the computer and insert it into your Raspberry Pi. The next time your Raspberry Pi is switched on, NOOBS will load and ask you to choose your operating system (**Figure A-1**).

◄ **Figure A-1:**
The NOOBS menu without any operating systems installed

NO PICTURE?

If you can't see Raspberry Pi on your display, check you are using the correct input. If your TV or monitor has more than one HDMI input, switch through each in turn using the 'Source' or 'Input' button until you see the NOOBS menu.

This is the NOOBS menu, a system which lets you choose the operating system to run on your Raspberry Pi. Two operating systems are included with NOOBS as standard: Raspbian, a version of the Debian Linux operating system tailored specifically for Raspberry Pi; and LibreELEC, a version of the Kodi Entertainment Centre software. If Raspberry Pi is connected to the network – either through a wired connection or using the 'Wifi networks (w)' option from the top bar of icons – you can also download and install other operating systems.

To begin installing an operating system, use the mouse to put a cross in the box to the left of Raspbian Full: point the cursor at the white box and click once with the left mouse button. When you've done so, you'll see that the 'Install (i)' menu icon is no longer greyed-out; this lets you know that your operating system is ready to install (**Figure A-2**).

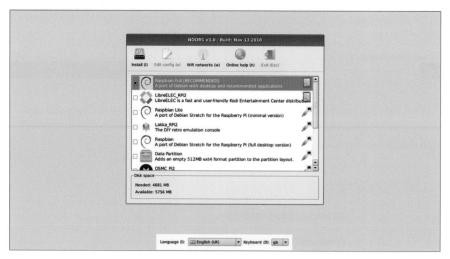

▲ **Figure A-2:** Choosing an operating system to install through NOOBS

Click the 'Install (i)' icon once with the left mouse button and you'll see a warning message telling you that installing the operating system will overwrite any data currently stored on the microSD card – not counting NOOBS itself, which stays intact. Click 'Yes' and the installation process will begin (**Figure 2-3**).

▲ **Figure A-3:** Installing the Raspbian operating system

The installation process can take anything from 10 to 30 minutes, depending on the speed of your microSD card. As the operating system is installed, progress is shown in a bar along the bottom of the window, you'll see a slide show highlighting some of its key features; you'll learn more about these, and Raspbian itself, in **Chapter 3, Using your Raspberry Pi**.

WARNING!

It's important that the installation isn't interrupted as this has a high likelihood of damaging the software, a process known as *data corruption*. Do not remove the microSD card or unplug the power cable while the operating system is being installed; if something does happen to interrupt the installation, unplug Raspberry Pi from its power supply, then hold down the **SHIFT** key on the keyboard as you connect Raspberry Pi to its power supply to bring the NOOBS menu back up. This is known as *recovery mode*, and is a great way to restore a Raspberry Pi whose software has been corrupted to working order again. It also allows you to enter the NOOBS menu after a successful installation, to reinstall the operating system, or install one of the other operating systems.

When the installation has finished, a window will pop up with an 'OK' button; click this and Raspberry Pi will restart into its freshly installed operating system. Note that the first time you boot into Raspbian, it can take a minute or two as it adjusts itself to make the best use of the free space on your microSD card. The next time you boot, things will go more quickly.

Appendix B

Installing and uninstalling software

Raspbian for Raspberry Pi comes with a selection of popular software packages, hand-picked by the Raspberry Pi Foundation, but these are not the only packages that will work on a Raspberry Pi. Using the following instructions, you can browse additional software, install it, and uninstall it again – expanding the capabilities of your Raspberry Pi.

The instructions in this appendix are on top of those in **Chapter 3, Using your Raspberry Pi**, which explains how to use the Recommended Software tool; if you haven't read that already, do so before using the methods described in this appendix.

CARD CAPACITY

Adding more software to your Raspberry Pi will take up space on your microSD card. A 16GB or larger card will let you install more software; to check whether the card you intend to use is compatible with Raspberry Pi, visit **rpf.io/sdcardlist**.

Browsing available software

To see and search the list of software packages available for Raspbian, using what are known as its *software repositories*, click the raspberry icon to load the menu, select the Preferences category, then click on Add/Remove Software. After a few seconds, the tool's window will appear.

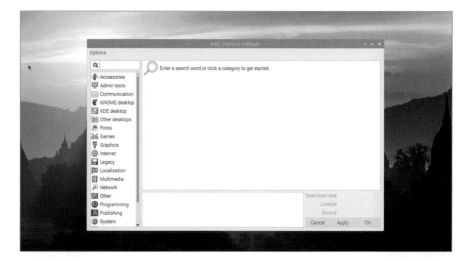

The left-hand side of the Add/Remove Software window contains a list of categories – the same categories that you find in the main menu when you click on the raspberry icon. Clicking on one will show you a list of the software available in that category. You can also enter a search term in the box at the top-left of the window, such as 'text editor' or 'game', and see a list of matching software packages from any category. Clicking on any package brings up additional information about it in the space to the bottom of the window.

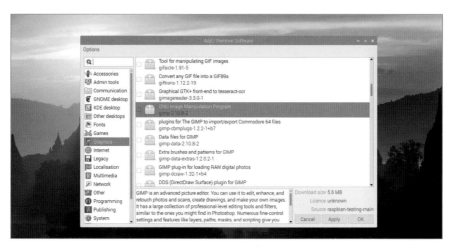

If the category you've chosen has lots of software packages available, it may take some time for the Add/Remove Software tool to finish working through the list.

Installing software

To select a package for installation, check the box next to it by clicking on it. You can install more than one package at once: just keep clicking to add more packages. The icon next to the package will change to an open box with a '+' symbol, to confirm that it's going to be installed.

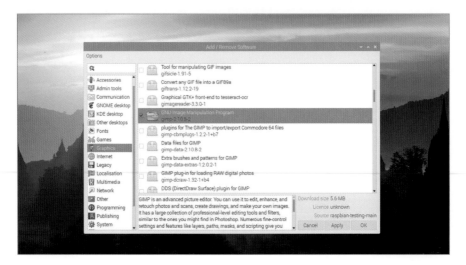

When you're happy with your choices, click either the OK or Apply button; the only difference is that OK will close the Add/Remove Software tool when your software is installed, while the Apply button leaves it open. You'll be asked to enter your password, to confirm your identity — you wouldn't want just anyone able to add or remove software from your Raspberry Pi, after all!

You may find that when you install a single package, other packages are installed alongside it; these are known as *dependencies*, packages that the software you chose to install needs to work – sound effect bundles for a game, for example, or a database to go with a web server.

Once the software is installed, you should be able to find it by clicking on the raspberry icon to load the menu and finding the software package's category. Be aware that the menu category isn't always the same as the category from the Add/Remove Software Tool, while some software doesn't have an entry in the menu at all; this software is known as *command-line software* and needs to be run at the Terminal. For more information on the command line and the Terminal, turn to **Appendix C, The command-line interface**.

Uninstalling software

To select a package for removal, or *uninstallation*, find it in the list of packages – the search function is handy here – and uncheck the box next to it by clicking on it. You can uninstall more than one package at once: just keep clicking to remove more packages. The icon next to the package will change to an open box next to a small recycle bin, to confirm that it's going to be uninstalled.

As before, you can click OK or Apply to begin uninstalling the selected software packages. You'll be asked to confirm your password, unless you did so within the last few minutes, and you may also be prompted to confirm that you want to remove any dependencies relating to your software package as well. When the uninstallation has finished, the software will disappear from the raspberry icon menu, but files you created using the software – pictures for a graphics package, for example, or saves for a game – won't be removed.

> ## WARNING!
>
> All software installed in Raspbian appears in Add/Remove Software, including software required for your Raspberry Pi to run. It's possible to remove enough packages that the desktop no longer loads. To avoid this, don't uninstall things unless you're sure you no longer need them. If it's already happened, reinstall Raspbian using the instructions in **Chapter 2, Getting started with your Raspberry Pi**, or reinstall NOOBS using **Appendix A**.

Appendix C
The command-line interface

W hile you can manage most of the software on a Raspberry Pi through the desktop, some can only be accessed using a text-based mode known as the *command-line interface (CLI)* in an application called Terminal. Most users will never need to use the CLI, but for those who want to learn more, this appendix offers a basic introduction.

> **MORE INFO**
>
> This appendix is not designed to be an exhaustive guide to the Linux command-line interface. For a more detailed look at using the CLI, visit **rpf.io/terminal** in a web browser.

Loading the Terminal

The CLI is accessed through the Terminal, a software package which loads what is technically known as a *virtual teletype (VTY) terminal*, a name dating back to the early days of computers when users issued commands via a large electromechanical typewriter rather than a keyboard and monitor. To load the Terminal package, click on the raspberry icon to load the menu, choose the Accessories category, then click on Terminal.

The Terminal window can be dragged around the desktop, resized, maximised, and minimised just like any other window. You can also make the writing in it bigger if it's hard to see, or smaller if you want to fit more in the window: click the Edit menu and choose Zoom In or Zoom Out respectively, or press and hold the **CTRL** key on the keyboard followed by **+** or **-**.

The prompt

The first thing you see in a Terminal is the *prompt*, which is waiting for your instructions. The prompt on a Raspberry Pi running Raspbian looks like this:

```
pi@raspberrypi:~ $
```

The first part of the prompt, **pi**, is your username; the second part, after the **@**, is the host name of the computer you're using, which is **raspberrypi** by default. After the '**:**' is a tilde, **~**, which is a shorthand way of referring to your home directory and represents your *current working directory (CWD)*. Finally, the **$** symbol indicates that your user is an *unprivileged user*, meaning that you need a password to carry out tasks like adding or removing software.

Getting around

Try typing the following then pressing the **ENTER** key:

```
cd Desktop
```

You'll see the prompt change to:

```
pi@raspberrypi:~/Desktop $
```

That shows you that your current working directory has changed: you were in your home directory before, indicated by the ~ symbol, and now you're in the **Desktop** subdirectory underneath your home directory. To do that, you used the **cd** command – *change directory*.

CORRECT CASE

Raspbian's command-line interface is case-sensitive, meaning that it matters when commands or names have upper- and lower-case letters. If you received a 'no such file or directory' message when you tried to change directories, check that you had a capital D at the start of Desktop.

There are four ways to go back to your home directory: try each in turn, changing back into the **Desktop** subdirectory each time. The first is:

```
cd ..
```

The .. symbols are another shortcut, this time for 'the directory above this one', also known as the *parent directory*. Because the directory above **Desktop** is your home directory, this returns you there. Change back into the **Desktop** subdirectory, and try the second way:

```
cd ~
```

This uses the ~ symbol, and literally means 'change into my home directory'. Unlike **cd ..**, which just takes you to the parent directory of whatever directory you're currently in, this command works from anywhere – but there's an easier way:

```
cd
```

Without being given the name of a directory, **cd** simply defaults to going back to your home directory. The final way to get back to your home directory is to type:

```
cd /home/pi
```

This uses what is called an *absolute path*, which will work regardless of the current working directory. So, like **cd** on its own or **cd ~**, this will return you to your home directory from wherever you are; unlike the other methods, though, it needs you to know your username.

Handling files

To practise working with files, change to the **Desktop** directory and type the following:

```
touch Test
```

You'll see a file called **Test** appear on the desktop. The **touch** command is normally used to update the date and time information on a file, but if – as in this case – the file doesn't exist, it creates it.

Try the following:

```
cp Test Test2
```

You'll see another file, **Test2**, appear on the desktop. This is a *copy* of the original file, identical in every way. Delete it by typing:

```
rm Test2
```

This *removes* the file, and you'll see it disappear.

> **WARNING!**
> Unlike deleting files using the graphical File Manager, which stores them in the Wastebasket
> for later retrieval, files deleted using **rm** are gone for good. Make sure you type with care!

Next, try:

```
mv Test Test2
```

This command *moves* the file, and you'll see your original **Test** file disappear and be replaced by **Test2**. The move command, **mv**, can be used like this to rename files.

When you're not on the desktop, though, you still need to be able to see what files are in a directory. Type:

```
ls
```

This command *lists* the contents of the current directory, or any other directory you give it. For more details, including listing any hidden files and reporting the sizes of files, try adding some switches:

```
ls -larth
```

These switches control the **ls** command: **l** switches its output into a long vertical list; **a** tells it to show all files and directories, including ones that would normally be hidden; **r** reverses the normal sort order; **t** sorts by modification time, which combined with **r** gives you the oldest files at the top of the list and the newest files at the bottom; and **h** uses human-readable file sizes, making the list easier to understand.

Running programs

Some programs can only be run at the command line, while others have both graphical and command-line interfaces. An example of the latter is the Raspberry Pi Software Configuration Tool, which you would normally load from the raspberry icon menu.

Type:

```
raspi-config
```

You'll be given an error telling you that the software can only be run as *root*, the superuser account on your Raspberry Pi. It will also tell you how to do that, by typing:

```
sudo raspi-config
```

The **sudo** part of the command means *switch-user do*, and tells Raspbian to run the command as the root user.

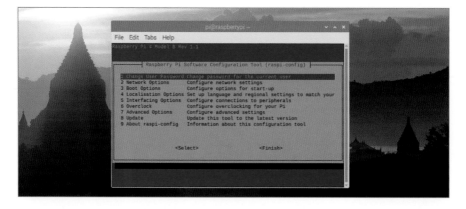

You'll only need to use **sudo** when a program needs elevated *privileges*, such as when it's installing or uninstalling software or adjusting system settings. A game, for example, should never be run using **sudo**.

Press the **TAB** key twice to select Finish and press **ENTER** to quit the Raspberry Pi Software Configuration Tool and return to the command-line interface. Finally, type:

```
exit
```

This will end your command-line interface session and close the Terminal app.

Using the TTYs

The Terminal application isn't the only way to use the command-line interface: you can also switch to one of a number of already-running terminals known as the *teletypes* or *TTYs*. Hold the **CTRL** and **ALT** keys on your keyboard and press the **F2** key to switch to 'tty2'.

```
Raspbian GNU/Linux 9 raspberrypi tty2
raspberrypi login:
```

You'll need to log in again with your username and password, after which you can use the command-line interface just like in the Terminal. Using these TTYs is handy when, for whatever reason, the main desktop interface isn't working.

To switch away from the TTY, press and hold **CTRL+ALT**, then press **F7**: the desktop will reappear. Press **CTRL+ALT+F2** again and you'll switch back to 'tty2' – and anything you were running in it will still be there.

Before switching again, type:

`exit`

Then press **CTRL+ALT+F7** to get back to the desktop. The reason for exiting before switching away from the TTY is that anybody with access to the keyboard can switch to a TTY, and if you're still logged in they'll be able to access your account without having to know your password!

Congratulations: you've taken your first steps in mastering the Raspbian command-line interface!

Appendix D
Further reading

The Official Raspberry Pi Beginner's Guide is designed to get you started with your Raspberry Pi, but it's by no means a complete look at everything you can do. The Raspberry Pi community is globe-spanning and vast, with people using them for everything from games and sensing applications to robotics and artificial intelligence, and there is a wealth of inspiration out there.

This appendix highlights some sources of project ideas, lesson plans, and other material which act as a great next step now you've worked your way through the *Beginner's Guide*.

The Raspberry Pi Blog

▷ **rpf.io/blog**

Your first stop for the latest news on all things Raspberry Pi, the official blog covers everything from new hardware launches and educational material to roundups of the best community projects, campaigns, and initiatives. If you want to keep up to date on all things Raspberry Pi, this is where you need to be.

Raspberry Pi Projects

▷ **rpf.io/projects**

The official Raspberry Pi Projects site offers step-by-step project tutorials in a range of categories, from making games and music to building your own website or Raspberry Pi-powered robot. Most projects are available in a variety of languages, too, and cover a range of difficulty levels suitable for everyone from absolute beginners to experienced makers.

Raspberry Pi Education

▸ **rpf.io/education**

The official Raspberry Pi Education site offers newsletters, online training, and projects with educators firmly in mind. The site also links to additional resources including the Picademy training programme, Code Club and CoderDojo volunteer-driven coding programmes, and global Raspberry Jam events.

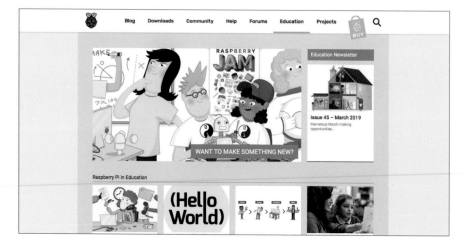

The Raspberry Pi Forums

▸ **rpf.io/forums**

The Raspberry Pi Forums are where Raspberry Pi fans can get together and chat about everything from beginner's issues to deeply technical topics — and there's even an 'off-topic' area for general chatting!

Community		Topics	Posts	Last post
General discussion		35678	281118	Re: RPi high school lab. B+ ... by tadcampagna Thu Apr 25, 2019 12:37 pm
Announcements Notifications about changes to the firmware, linux kernel and Raspbian.		4	4	New "gpio" config command by PhilE Thu Mar 22, 2018 1:12 pm
Other languages Community discussion in languages other than English		16244	84206	Re: Wifi fluctuant sur pi3 by epoch1970 Thu Apr 25, 2019 11:13 am
User groups and events		711	2780	Re: Beijing area by masafumi_ohta Tue Apr 16, 2019 2:18 am
The MagPi The Raspberry Pi community magazine - feedback, requests and discussion!		202	1226	Re: Back to the future by MrEngman Thu Apr 25, 2019 9:48 am

The MagPi Magazine

▸ **magpi.cc**

The official Raspberry Pi magazine, The MagPi is a glossy monthly publication which covers everything from tutorials and guides to reviews and news, supported in no small part by the worldwide Raspberry Pi community. Copies are available in all good newsagents and supermarkets, and can also be downloaded digitally free of charge under the Creative Commons licence. The MagPi also publishes the Essentials series of 'bookazines', which address specific individual topics – from using the command line to building your own electronics projects – in a friendly and easy-to-follow format. As with the magazine itself, they're available to buy in printed format or to download for free under the Creative Commons licence.

Hello World Magazine

▸ **helloworld.cc**

Published three times a year, Hello World is available free of charge for UK-based teachers, volunteers, and librarians. For everyone else, free digital copies can be downloaded under the Creative Commons licence, and subscriptions to the print version are available commercially.

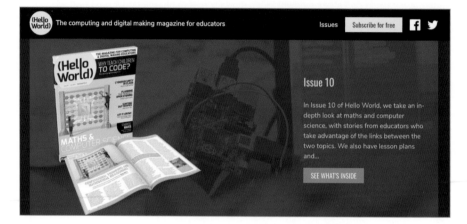

HackSpace Magazine

▸ **hsmag.cc**

Aimed at a broader audience than The MagPi, HackSpace Magazine takes a look at the maker community with hardware and software reviews, tutorials, and interviews. If you're interested in broadening your horizons beyond Raspberry Pi, HackSpace Magazine is a great place to start – it can be found in print at supermarkets and newsagents or downloaded for free in digital form.

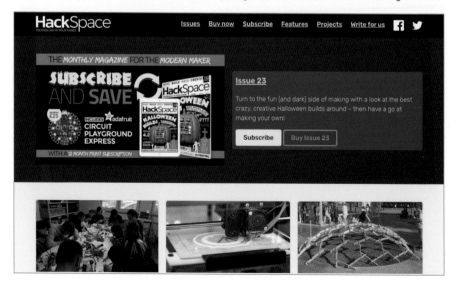

Appendix E
Raspberry Pi Configuration Tool

The Raspberry Pi Configuration Tool is a powerful package for adjusting numerous settings on your Raspberry Pi, from the interfaces available to programs to controlling it over a network. It can be a little daunting to newcomers, though, so this appendix will walk you through each of the settings in turn and explain their purposes.

You can load the Raspberry Pi Configuration Tool from the raspberry icon menu, under the Preferences category. It can also be run from the command-line interface or Terminal using the command **raspi-config**. The layouts of the command-line version and the graphical version are different, with options appearing in different categories, depending on which version you use; this appendix is based on the graphical version.

> ## WARNING!
>
> Unless you know you need a particular setting changed, it's best to leave the Raspberry Pi Configuration Tool alone. If you're adding new hardware to your Raspberry Pi, such as an audio HAT or a Camera Module, the instructions will tell you which setting to change; otherwise, the default settings should generally be left alone.

System tab

The System tab holds options which control various Raspbian system settings.

■ **Password:** Click the 'Change Password...' button to set a new password for your current user account. By default this is the 'pi' account.

■ **Hostname:** The name by which a Raspberry Pi identifies itself on networks. If you have more than one Raspberry Pi on the same network, they must each have a unique name of their own.

■ **Boot:** Setting this to 'To Desktop' (the default) loads the familiar Raspbian desktop; setting it to 'To CLI' loads the command-line interface as described in **Appendix C, The Command-Line Interface**.

■ **Auto Login:** When 'As current user' is ticked (the default), Raspbian will load the desktop without needing you to type in your user name and password.

■ **Network at Boot:** When 'Wait for network' is ticked, Raspbian will not load until it has a working network connection.

■ **Splash Screen:** When set to 'enabled' (the default), Raspbian's boot messages are hidden behind a graphical splash screen.

Display tab

The Display tab holds settings which control how the screen is displayed.

■ **Underscan:** This setting controls whether or not the video output on Raspberry Pi includes black bars around its edges, to compensate for the frame of many TVs. If you see black bars, set this to 'Disabled'; if not, leave it on 'Enabled.'

■ **Composite Video:** This controls the composite video output available on the combined audio-video (AV) jack, when used with a tip-ring-ring-sleeve (TRRS) adapter. If you want to use the composite video output instead of HDMI, set this to 'Enabled'; otherwise, leave it disabled.

■ **Screen Blanking:** This option enables you turn screen blanking (the timeout which turns the display off after a few minutes) on and off.

Interfaces tab

The Interfaces tab holds settings which control the hardware interfaces available on Raspberry Pi.

■ **Camera:** Enables or disables the Camera Serial Interface (CSI), for use with a Raspberry Pi Camera Module.

■ **SSH:** Enables/disables the Secure Shell (SSH) interface; it allows you to open a command-line interface on Raspberry Pi from another computer on your network using an SSH client.

■ **VNC:** Enables/disables the Virtual Network Computing (VNC) interface; it allows you to view the desktop on Raspberry Pi from another computer on your network using a VNC client.

■ **SPI:** Enables or disables the Serial Peripheral Interface (SPI), used to control some hardware add-ons which connect to the GPIO pins.

■ **I2C:** Enables or disables the Inter-Integrated Circuit (I²C) interface, used to control some hardware add-ons which connect to the GPIO pins.

■ **Serial Port:** Enables or disables Raspberry Pi's serial port, available on the GPIO pins.

■ **Serial Console:** Enables or disables the serial console, a command-line interface available on the serial port. This option is only available if the Serial Port setting above is set to Enabled.

■ **1-Wire:** Enables or disables the 1-Wire interface, used to control some hardware add-ons which connect to the GPIO pins.

■ **Remote GPIO:** Enables or disables a network service which allows you to control Raspberry Pi's GPIO pins from another computer on your network using the GPIO Zero library. More information on remote GPIO is available from **gpiozero.readthedocs.io**.

Performance tab

The Performance tab holds settings which control how much memory is available and how fast Raspberry Pi's processor runs.

■ **Overclock:** Allows you to choose from a range of settings that increase the performance of your Raspberry Pi at the cost of increased power usage, heat generation, and possible decreased overall lifespan. Not available on all models of Raspberry Pi.

■ **GPU Memory:** Allows you to set the amount of memory reserved for use by Raspberry Pi's graphics processor. Values higher than the default may improve performance for complicated 3D rendering and general-purpose GPU (GPGPU) tasks at the cost of reducing the memory available to Raspbian; lower values may improve performance for memory-intensive tasks at the cost of making 3D rendering, camera, and selected video playback features perform more slowly or become unavailable.

■ **Overlay File System:** Allows you to lock Raspberry Pi's file system down so that changes only get made to a virtual RAM disk rather than being written to the mircoSD card, so you go back to a clean state whenever you reboot.

Localisation tab

The Localisation tab holds settings which control which region your Raspberry Pi is designed to operate in, including keyboard layout settings.

■ **Locale:** Allows you to choose your locale, a system setting which includes language, country, and character set. Please note that changing the language here will only change the displayed language in applications for which a translation is available.

■ **Timezone:** Allows you to choose your regional time zone, selecting an area of the world followed by the closest city. If your Raspberry Pi is connected to the network but the clock is showing the wrong time, it's usually caused by the wrong time zone being selected.

■ **Keyboard:** Allows you to choose your keyboard type, language, and layout. If you find your keyboard types the wrong letters or symbols, you can correct it here.

■ **WiFi Country:** Allows you to set your country for radio regulation purposes. Make sure to select the country in which your Raspberry Pi is being used: selecting a different country may make it impossible to connect to nearby WiFi access points and can be a breach of broadcasting law. A country must be set before the WiFi radio can be used.

Appendix F
Raspberry Pi specifications

The various components and features of a computer are known as its specifications, and a look at the specifications gives you the information you need to compare two computers. These specifications can seem confusing at first, are highly technical, and you don't need to know them to use a Raspberry Pi, but they are included here for the curious reader.

Raspberry Pi 4 Model B's system-on-chip is a Broadcom BCM2711B0, which you'll see written on its metal lid if you look closely enough. This features four 64-bit ARM Cortex-A72 central processing unit (CPU) cores, each running at 1.5GHz (1.5 thousand million cycles per second), and a Broadcom VideoCore VI (Six) graphics processing unit (GPU) running at 500MHz (500 million cycles per second) for video tasks and for 3D rendering tasks such as games.

The system-on-chip is connected to 1GB, 2GB, or 4GB (one, two, or four thousand million bytes) of LPDDR4 (Low-Power Double-Data-Rate 4) RAM (random-access memory), which runs at 3,200MHz (three thousand two hundred million cycles per second). This memory is shared between the central processor and the graphics processor. The microSD card slot supports up to 512GB (512 thousand million bytes) of storage.

The Ethernet port supports up to gigabit (1000Mbps, 1000-Base-T) connections, while the radio supports 802.11ac WiFi networks running on the 2.4GHz and 5GHz frequency bands, Bluetooth 5.0, and Bluetooth Low Energy (BLE) connections.

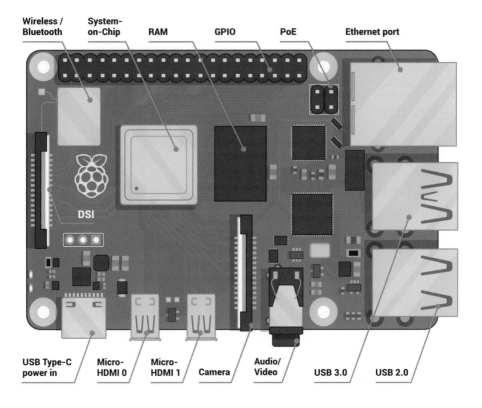

Broken down into a bullet list, those specifications look like this:

■ **CPU:** 64-bit quad-core ARM Cortex-A72 at 1.5GHz

■ **GPU:** VideoCore VI at 500MHz

■ **RAM:** 1GB, 2GB, or 4GB of LPDDR4

■ **Networking:** Gigabit Ethernet, dual-band 802.11ac, Bluetooth 5.0, Bluetooth Low Energy

■ **Audio/Video Outputs:** 3.5mm analogue AV jack, 2 × micro-HDMI 2.0

■ **Peripheral Connectivity:** 2 × USB 2.0 ports, 2 × USB 3.0 ports, Camera Serial Interface, Display Serial Interface (DSI)

■ **Storage:** microSD, up to 512GB

■ **Power:** 5 volts at 3 amps via USB Type-C

■ **Extras:** 40-pin GPIO header, Power over Ethernet compatibility (with additional hardware)

Appendix G
Raspberry Pi 4 Model B Safety and User Guide

Raspberry Pi

Designed and distributed by
Raspberry Pi Trading Ltd
Maurice Wilkes Building
Cowley Road
Cambridge
CB4 0DS
UK
www.raspberrypi.org

Raspberry Pi Regulatory compliance and safety information

Product name: Raspberry Pi 4
Model B 1GB, 2GB + 4GB variants

IMPORTANT: PLEASE RETAIN THIS INFORMATION FOR FUTURE REFERENCE.

Warnings

- Any external power supply used with the Raspberry Pi shall comply with relevant regulations and standards applicable in the country of intended use. The power supply should provide 5V DC and a minimum rated current of 3A.

Instructions for safe use

- This product should not be overclocked.
- Do not expose this product to water or moisture, and do not place it on a conductive surface whilst in operation.
- Do not expose this product to heat from any source; it is designed for reliable operation at normal room temperatures.
- Operate this product in a well-ventilated environment, and do not cover it during use.
- Place this product on a stable, flat, non-conductive surface while in use, and do not let it contact conductive items.
- Take care while handling this product to avoid mechanical or electrical damage to the printed circuit board and connectors.
- Avoid handling this product while it is powered. Only handle by the edges to minimize the risk of electrostatic discharge damage.
- Any peripheral or equipment used with the Raspberry Pi should comply with relevant standards for the country of use and be marked accordingly to ensure that safety and performance requirements are met. Such equipment includes, but is not limited to, keyboards, monitors, and mice.

For all compliance certificates and numbers, please visit www.raspberrypi.org/compliance.

汉语

Raspberry Pi 4 代B型1GB, 2GB + 4GB
重要提示：请保留此信息以供将来参考。
警告

- Raspberry Pi 使用的任何外置电源应符合所在国家的相关法规和标准。 电源应提供 5V DC 和 3A 最小额定电流。
- 安全使用说明
- 此产品不可超频。
- 请勿将本产品暴露在水或潮湿环境中；当其运行时，请勿将其置于导电表面上。
- 请勿将此产品暴露于任何热源；此产品仅适合在正常室温中使用，以确保可靠运行。
- 在通风良好的环境中运行此产品，在使用过程中请勿覆盖。
- 使用时，请将本产品放在稳定、平坦、绝缘的表面上，请勿让它接触导电物品。
- 拿放本产品时请小心，以免对

印刷电路板和连接器造成机械或电气损坏。

■ 本产品通电时应避免接触、拿放。拿放时应只接触产品的边缘，以最大限度地降低静电放电损坏的风险。

■ Raspberry Pi使用的任何外设或设备应符合使用国家的相关标准，并进行相应标记，以确保满足安全和性能要求。

如需查询所有合规证书及编号，请访问 www.raspberrypi.org/compliance 。

Čeština

Raspberry Pi 4 Model B 1GB, 2GB + 4GB

DŮLEŽITÉ: TUTO INFORMACI SI PONECHTE PRO POUŽITÍ V BUDOUCNU.

Varování

■ Každý externí napájecí zdroj použitý s Raspberry Pi musí splňovat příslušné předpisy a normy platné v zemi určení. Napájecí zdroj by měl poskytovat stejnosměrné napětí 5V a minimální jmenovitý proud 3A.

Pokyny pro bezpečné používání

■ Tento výrobek by neměl být přetaktován.

■ Výrobek nevystavujte vodě ani vlhkosti a za provozu ho neumisťujte na vodivý povrch.

■ Výrobek nevystavujte teplu z jakéhokoli zdroje; je navržen pro spolehlivý provoz při normálních pokojových teplotách.

■ Výrobek používejte v dobře větraném prostředí a za provozu ho nepřikrývejte.

■ Výrobek při používání ponechte na stabilním, plochém a nevodivém povrchu a zabraňte jeho dotyku s vodivými předměty.

■ Při manipulaci s výrobkem dbejte na to, abyste zabránili mechanickému nebo elektrickému poškození desky plošných spojů a konektorů.

■ Vyvarujte se manipulace s výrobkem, když je napájen. K manipulaci používejte pouze okraje, abyste minimalizovali riziko poškození elektrostatickým výbojem.

■ Veškerá periferní a další zařízení používaná s Raspberry Pi by měla být v souladu s příslušnými normami země použití a měla by být odpovídajícím způsobem označena, aby se zajistilo, že splňují požadavky na bezpečnost a výkon.

Všechna osvědčení o shodě a čísla najdete na www.raspberrypi.org/compliance.

Dansk

Raspberry Pi 4 Model B 1GB, 2GB + 4GB

VIGTIGT: OPBEVAR DENNE INFORMATION FOR FREMTIDIG REFERENCE.

Advarsler

■ Eksterne strømforsyninger, der anvendes til Raspberry Pi skal være i overensstemmelse med relevante bestemmelser og standarder, som er gældende i det land, hvor anvendelsen er tiltænkt. Strømforsyningen skal give 5 V jævnstrøm og en nominel strømstyrke på mindst 3 A.

Instruktioner for sikker brug

■ Dette produkt må ikke overophedes.

■ Udsæt ikke dette produkt for vand eller fugt, og sæt det ikke på en ledende overflade under drift.

■ Udsæt ikke dette produkt for varme fra nogen kilder; det er designet til pålidelig drift ved normal stuetemperatur.

■ Anvend dette produkt i et godt ventileret miljø, og tildæk det ikke under brug.

■ Anbring dette produkt på en stabil, flad og ikke-ledende overflade under brug, og lad det ikke komme i berøring med ledende genstande.

■ Vær forsigtig ved håndtering af dette produkt for at undgå mekanisk eller elektrisk beskadigelse af printkort og stik.

■ Undgå håndtering af dette produkt, mens det er tændt. Må kun håndteres ved at holde i kanterne for at minimere risikoen for skader ved elektrostatisk udladning.

■ Alt perifert udstyr eller udstyr, der anvendes til Raspberry Pi skal overholde relevante standarder i landet for anvendelse og mærkes i overensstemmelse hermed for at sikre, at kravene for sikkerhed og ydeevne er opfyldt.

For alle overensstemmelsescertifikater og numre, gå på www.raspberrypi.org/compliance.

Nederlands

Raspberry Pi 4 Model B 1GB, 2GB + 4GB

BELANGRIJK: BEWAAR DEZE INFORMATIE VOOR TOEKOMSTIGE VERWIJZING.

Waarschuwingen

■ Elke externe voeding die met de Raspberry Pi wordt gebruikt, moet voldoen aan de relevante voorschriften en normen die van toepassing zijn in het land van het beoogde gebruik. De voeding moet 5V DC en een minimale nominale stroom van 3A leveren.

Instructies voor veilig gebruik

■ Dit product mag niet overklokt worden.

■ Stel dit product niet bloot aan water of vocht en plaats het tijdens gebruik niet op een geleidend oppervlak.

■ Stel dit product niet bloot aan warmte van welke bron dan ook; het is ontworpen voor betrouwbare werking bij normale kamertemperatuur.

■ Gebruik dit product in een goed

geventileerde omgeving en dek het niet af tijdens gebruik.

■ Plaats dit product tijdens het gebruik op een stabiel, plat, niet-geleidend oppervlak en laat het niet in contact komen met geleidende items.

■ Wees voorzichtig met het gebruik van dit product om mechanische of elektrische schade aan de printplaat en connectoren te voorkomen.

■ Gebruik dit product niet terwijl het wordt gevoed. Alleen aan de randen vasthouden om het risico op schade door elektrostatische ontlading te minimaliseren.

■ Alle randapparatuur of apparatuur die met de Raspberry Pi wordt gebruikt, moet voldoen aan de relevante normen voor het land van gebruik en dienovereenkomstig worden gemarkeerd om ervoor te zorgen dat wordt voldaan aan de veiligheids- en prestatie-eisen. Ga naar www.raspberrypi.org/compliance.

Suomi

Raspberry Pi 4 Malli B 1GB, 2GB + 4GB
TÄRKEÄÄ: SÄILYTÄ NÄMÄ TIEDOT MYÖHEMMÄN KÄYTÖN VARALTA.
Varoituksia

■ Kaikkien ulkoisen Raspberry Pi -laitteessa käytettyjen virtalähteiden on noudatettava käyttömaassa sovellettavia asiaankuuluvia asetuksia ja standardeja. Virtalähteen virran on oltava 5V DC minimin nimellisvirran ollessa 3A.
Ohjeet turvallista käyttöä varten

■ Tätä tuotetta ei saa ylikuormittaa.

■ Älä altista tätä tuotetta vedelle tai kosteudelle, äläkä aseta sitä johtavalle pinnalle sen ollessa toiminnassa.

■ Älä altista tätä tuotetta

mistään lähteestä aiheutuvalle kuumuudelle; se on suunniteltu luotettavaa toimintaa varten normaaleissa huonelämpötiloissa.

■ Käytä tätä tuotetta hyvin ilmastoidussa lämpötilassa, äläkä peitä sitä käytön aikana.

■ Aseta tämä tuote vakaalle, tasaiselle, ei-johtavalle pinnalle sen ollessa käytössä, äläkä anna sen koskettaa johtavia kohteita.

■ Noudata varovaisuutta tätä tuotetta käsiteltäessä mekaanisen tai sähköisen vaurioitumisen estämiseksi painetulle piirilevylle ja liittimille.

■ Vältä tämän tuotteen käsittelyä sen ollessa kytkettynä virtalähteeseen. Käsittele vain reunoista sähköstaattisen purkautumisen vaaran minimoimiseksi.

■ Kaikkien Raspberry Pi -laitteiden kanssa käytettävien oheislaitteiden ja muiden laitteiden on oltava käyttömaan asianmukaisten standardien mukaisia, ja niiden on oltava merkittyjä sen varmistamiseksi, että turvallisuus ja suorituskykyvaatimukset täytetään.
Lisätietojen saamiseksi kaikista vaatimustenmukaisuussertifikaateista vieraile verkkosivustolla www.raspberrypi.org/compliance.

Français

Raspberry Pi 4 Modèle B 1GB, 2GB + 4GB
IMPORTANT: VEUILLEZ CONSERVER CETTE INFORMATION POUR VOUS Y REPORTER ULTÉRIEUREMENT.
Avertissements

■ Toute alimentation électrique externe utilisée avec le Raspberry Pi doit être conforme aux réglementations et normes applicables dans le pays d'utilisation. L'alimentation

électrique doit fournir 5 V CC et un courant nominal minimum de 3 A.
Consignes pour une utilisation en toute sécurité

■ Ce produit ne doit pas être utilisé à une vitesse supérieure à celle prévue pour son usage.

■ N'exposez pas ce produit à l'eau ou à l'humidité et ne le placez pas sur une surface conductrice pendant le fonctionnement.

■ N'exposez pas ce produit à la chaleur quelle qu'en soit la source; il est conçu pour un fonctionnement fiable à des températures ambiantes normales.

■ Faites fonctionner ce produit dans un environnement bien ventilé et ne le couvrez pas pendant l'utilisation.

■ Placez ce produit sur une surface stable, plane et non conductrice pendant son utilisation et ne le laissez pas en contact avec des éléments conducteurs.

■ Faites attention lors de la manipulation de ce produit pour éviter tout dommage mécanique ou électrique au niveau de la carte de circuit imprimé et des connecteurs.

■ Évitez de manipuler ce produit lorsqu'il est sous tension. Ne manipulez que par les bords afin de minimiser les risques de dommages dus aux décharges électrostatiques.

■ Tout périphérique ou équipement utilisé avec le Raspberry Pi doit être conforme aux normes applicables dans le pays d'utilisation et être marqué en conséquence pour garantir la sécurité et les performances.
Pour tous les certificats et numéros de conformité, veuillez consulter www.raspberrypi.org/compliance

Deutsch

Raspberry Pi 4 Modell B 1GB, 2GB + 4GB
WICHTIG: BITTE BEWAHREN SIE DIESE INFORMATIONEN FÜR ZUKÜNFTIGE REFERENZ.
Achtung

- Jedes externe Netzteil, das mit dem Raspberry Pi verwendet wird, muss den einschlägigen Vorschriften und Normen entsprechen, die im Bestimmungsland gelten. Die Stromversorgung sollte 5 V Gleichstrom und einen minimalen Nennstrom von 3 A liefern.
- Anweisungen für die sichere Verwendung
- Dieses Produkt sollte nicht übertaktet werden.
- Setzen Sie dieses Produkt nicht Wasser oder Feuchtigkeit aus und stellen Sie es während des Betriebs nicht auf eine leitfähige Oberfläche.
- Setzen Sie dieses Produkt keiner Wärmequelle aus. Es ist für einen zuverlässigen Betrieb bei normalen Raumtemperaturen ausgelegt.
- Betreiben Sie dieses Produkt in einer gut belüfteten Umgebung und decken Sie es während des Gebrauchs nicht ab.
- Stellen Sie dieses Produkt während des Gebrauchs auf eine stabile, flache, nicht leitende Oberfläche und lassen Sie es nicht mit leitfähigen Gegenständen in Berührung kommen.
- Seien Sie vorsichtig beim Umgang mit diesem Produkt, um mechanische oder elektrische Schäden an der Leiterplatte und den Anschlüssen zu vermeiden.
- Vermeiden Sie die Handhabung dieses Produkts während der Stromversorgung. Produkt nur an den Rändern anfassen, um das Risiko von elektrostatischen Entladungsschäden zu minimieren.
- Alle Peripheriegeräte oder Geräte, die mit dem Raspberry Pi verwendet werden, müssen den geltenden Normen für das jeweilige Land entsprechen und entsprechend gekennzeichnet sein, um zu gewährleisten, dass die Sicherheits- und Leistungsanforderungen erfüllt werden.

Alle Konformitätszertifikate und -nummern finden Sie auf www. raspberrypi.org/compliance .

Italiano

Raspberry Pi 4 Model B 1GB, 2GB + 4GB

IMPORTANTE: CONSERVARE QUESTE INFORMAZIONI PER RIFERIMENTO FUTURO.
Avvisi

- Tutti gli alimentatori esterni utilizzati con il Raspberry Pi devono essere conformi alle normative e agli standard pertinenti applicabili nel paese di utilizzo previsto. L'alimentatore utilizzato dovrà fornire 5 V CC e una corrente nominale minima di 3 A.

Istruzioni per l'utilizzo in sicurezza

- Questo prodotto non deve essere overcloccato.
- Non esporre questo prodotto all'acqua o all'umidità e non collocarlo su una superficie conduttiva mentre è in funzione.
- Non esporre questo prodotto a fonti di calore. Il prodotto è progettato per un funzionamento affidabile solo alla normale temperatura ambiente.
- Utilizzare questo prodotto in un ambiente ben ventilato e non coprirlo durante l'uso.
- Per l'uso, collocare questo prodotto su una superficie stabile, piana e non conduttiva. Evitare che venga in contatto con oggetti conduttivi.
- Durante l'uso o lo spostamento del prodotto prestare attenzione ad evitare danni meccanici o elettrici al circuito stampato e ai connettori.
- Evitare di maneggiare questo prodotto mentre è alimentato. Afferrare solo dai bordi per ridurre al minimo il rischio di danni da scariche elettrostatiche.
- Tutte le periferiche e le apparecchiature utilizzate con il Raspberry Pi devono essere conformi agli standard pertinenti per il paese di utilizzo ed essere dotate del relativo marchio a garanzia della conformità con i requisiti di sicurezza e prestazioni necessari.

Per informazioni su numeri e certificati di conformità, visitare www.raspberrypi.org/compliance.

日本語

Raspberry Pi 4 モデルB 1GB, 2GB + 4GB
重要: 将来参照できるようこの情報は保管しておいてください。
警告

- Raspberry Pi と共に使用する外部電源は使用対象国内の規制や基準に準拠したものにしてください。 電源の出力は 5V DC で最低定格電流が 3A でなければなりません。

安全な使用のための説明

- 本製品をオーバークロックしてはなりません。
- 本製品を水や湿気にさらしたり、動作中に導電性の面に置いてはなりません。
- 本製品をどんな熱源からの熱にもさらさないでください。本製品は通常の室温で動作するように設計されています。
- 本製品は通気性の良い環境で使用し、使用中に密閉しない

でください。
- 本製品の使用中は本製品を平らな安定した非導電性の面に置き、導電性の物に接触させないでください。
- 本製品を扱う際は慎重に取り扱い、プリント基板およびコネクター類への物理的または電気的損傷を避けてください。
- 電源が入っている状態で本製品に触れることは避けてください。静電放電による損傷のリスクを最小限にするため、持つ際は端を持ってください。
- 安全と性能の要件を満たすため、Raspberry Pi と共に使用する周辺機器または装置は使用国内の規制や基準に準拠したものにし、該当する表記のあるものにしてください。

すべての順守証明書および番号については www.raspberrypi.org/compliance を参照してください

한국어

Raspberry Pi 4 모델B 1GB, 2GB + 4GB
중요: 추후 참조를 위해 이 정보를 보관하십시오.
경고
- Raspberry Pi 와 함께 사용되는 모든 외부 전원 공급 장치는, 해당 국가에서 적용되는 관련 규정 및 표준을 준수해야합니다. 전원 공급 장치는 5V DC, 최소 정격 전류 3A를 공급해야 합니다.

안전한 사용을 위한 지침
- 본 제품을 '오버클럭' 해서는 안됩니다.
- 본 제품을 물이나 습기에 노출시키지 말고, 작동 중에 전도성 표면 위에 놓지 마십시오.
- 본 제품을 모든 소스의 열에 노출시키지 마십시오. 일반적인 실내 온도에서 안정적인 작동을 하도록 설계되었습니다.
- 본 제품을 통풍이 잘되는 환경에서 사용하고, 사용

중에는 덮지 마십시오.
- 이 제품을 사용하는 동안 안정적이고 편평한 비전도성 표면에 놓고, 전도성 물품에 접촉시키지 마십시오.
- 인쇄회로기판 및 커넥터의 기계적 또는 전기적 손상을 방지하기 위해, 본 제품을 취급할 때 주의하십시오.
- 전원이 공급되는 동안에는 본 제품을 다루지 마십시오. 정전기로 인한 손상 위험을 최소화하기 위해 가장자리만 잡으십시오.
- Raspberry Pi 와 함께 사용되는 모든 주변 장치 또는 장비는, 해당 사용 국가의 관련 표준을 준수해야 하며 또한 안전 및 성능 요구사항을 충족하도록 표시해야 합니다.

모든 준수 인증서 및 번호는, 다음 사이트를 참조하십시오. www.raspberrypi.org/compliance.

Polski

Raspberry Pi 4 Model B 1GB, 2GB + 4GB
WAŻNE: PROSIMY ZACHOWAĆ TE INFORMACJE NA PRZYSZŁOŚĆ.
Ostrzeżenia
- Wszelkie zewnętrzne źródła zasilania używane z Raspberry Pi powinny być zgodne z odpowiednimi przepisami i normami obowiązującymi w kraju przeznaczenia. Zasilacz powinien zapewniać napięcie 5V DC i minimalny prąd znamionowy 3A.

Instrukcje bezpiecznego użytkowania
- Ten produkt nie powinien być przetaktowany.
- Nie należy wystawiać tego produktu na działanie wody ani wilgoci, ani umieszczać go na powierzchni przewodzącej podczas pracy.
- Nie należy wystawiać tego produktu na działanie ciepła z jakiegokolwiek źródła; produkt zaprojektowano tak, aby działał

niezawodnie w normalnej temperaturze pokojowej.
- Używać w dobrze wentylowanym otoczeniu i nie zakrywać podczas użytkowania.
- Podczas użytkowania należy umieścić produkt na stabilnej, płaskiej, nieprzewodzącej powierzchni i nie dopuścić do kontaktu z przedmiotami przewodzącymi prąd.
- Należy zachować ostrożność podczas obchodzenia się z produktem, aby uniknąć mechanicznego lub elektrycznego uszkodzenia płyty z obwodami drukowanymi i złączy.
- Nie należy przenosić produktu, gdy jest podłączony do zasilania. Trzymać wyłącznie za krawędzie, aby zminimalizować ryzyko uszkodzenia w wyniku wyładowań elektrostatycznych.
- Wszelkie urządzenia peryferyjne lub sprzęt używany z Raspberry Pi powinny być zgodne z odpowiednimi normami dla kraju użytkowania i być odpowiednio oznakowane, aby zapewnić spełnienie wymagań bezpieczeństwa i wymogów eksploatacyjnych.

Wszystkie certyfikaty zgodności i numery można znaleźć na stronie www.raspberrypi.org/compliance.

Português do Brasil

Raspberry Pi 4 Modelo B 1GB, 2GB + 4GB
IMPORTANTE: POR FAVOR, GUARDE ESTAS INFORMAÇÕES PARA REFERÊNCIA FUTURA.
Avisos
- Qualquer fonte de alimentação externa usada com o Raspberry Pi deve cumprir os regulamentos e normas aplicáveis no país de utilização. A fonte de alimentação deve fornecer 5V CC e uma corrente nominal mínima de 3A.

Instruções para o uso seguro

■ Este produto não deve ser usado em overclock.

■ Não exponha este produto à água ou à umidade, e não o coloque em uma superfície condutora durante a operação.

■ Não exponha este produto ao calor de qualquer fonte; Ele é projetado para operação confiável à temperatura ambiente.

■ Opere este produto em um ambiente bem ventilado e não o cubra durante o uso.

■ Coloque este produto em uma superfície estável, plana e não condutora durante o uso, e não deixe que entre em contato com dispositivos que conduzem eletricidade.

■ Tome cuidado ao manusear este produto para evitar danos mecânicos ou elétricos à placa de circuito impresso e aos conectores.

■ Evite manusear este produto enquanto estiver ligado. Somente manuseie pelas bordas (laterais) para minimizar o risco de dano por descarga eletrostática.

■ Qualquer periférico ou equipamento usado com o Raspberry Pi deve cumprir os padrões de fabricação e uso relevantes para o país e assim garantir que os requisitos de segurança e desempenho sejam atendidos.

Para todos os certificados conformidade e números, visite www.raspberrypi.org/compliance.

Русский

Raspberry Pi 4 Модель B 1GB, 2GB + 4GB
ВАЖНО: СОХРАНИТЕ ЭТУ ИНФОРМАЦИЮ ДЛЯ БУДУЩЕГО ИСПОЛЬЗОВАНИЯ.
Внимание!

■ Любой внешний источник питания, используемый с Raspberry Pi, должен соответствовать соответствующим нормам и стандартам, применяемым в стране предполагаемого использования. Источник питания должен обеспечивать 5 В постоянного тока и минимальный номинальный ток 3 A.

Инструкции по безопасному использованию

■ Этот продукт не должен использоваться вопреки нормативам производителя.

■ Не подвергайте этот продукт воздействию воды или влаги и не размещайте его на проводящей поверхности во время работы.

■ Не подвергайте этот продукт воздействию тепла из любого источника; он предназначен для надежной работы при нормальной комнатной температуре.

■ Эксплуатируйте этот продукт в хорошо проветриваемой среде и не накрывайте его во время использования.

■ Поместите этот продукт на устойчивую, плоскую, непроводящую поверхность во время использования и не позволяйте ему контактировать с проводящими изделиями.

■ Соблюдайте осторожность при обращении с этим продуктом, чтобы избежать механического или электрического повреждения печатной платы и разъемов.

■ Избегайте обращения с этим продуктом во время его питания. Используйте только края, чтобы свести к минимуму риск повреждения электростатического разряда.

■ Любое периферийное устройство или оборудование,

используемое с Raspberry Pi, должно соответствовать соответствующим стандартам для страны использования и быть соответствующим образом маркировано для обеспечения соблюдения требований безопасности и производительности.

Для всех сертификатов соответствия и номеров, пожалуйста, посетите www.raspberrypi.org/compliance .

Español

Raspberry Pi 4 Modelo B 1GB, 2GB + 4GB
IMPORTANTE: POR FAVOR CONSERVE ESTA INFORMACIÓN PARA FUTURA REFERENCIA.
Advertencias

■ Cualquier fuente de alimentación externa utilizada con la Raspberry Pi deberá cumplir con las correspondientes regulaciones y normas aplicables en el país de uso previsto. La fuente de alimentación debe proporcionar 5V DC y una corriente nominal mínima de 3A.

Instrucciones para un uso seguro

■ Este producto no debe ser usado con una frecuencia de reloj superior a la nominal. (No se debe overclockear).

■ No exponga este producto al agua o a la humedad, y no lo coloque sobre una superficie conductora mientras está en funcionamiento.

■ No exponga este producto a ningún tipo de fuente de calor; está diseñado para un funcionamiento fiable a temperatura ambiente normal.

■ Utilice este producto en un ambiente bien ventilado, y no lo cubra durante el uso.

■ Coloque este producto sobre una superficie estable, plana y no conductora mientras esté en uso, y no permita que entre en contacto con elementos conductores.

■ Tenga cuidado al manipular este producto para evitar daños mecánicos o eléctricos en la placa de circuito impreso y en los conectores.

■ Evite manipular este producto mientras está encendido. Sujételo solo por los bordes para minimizar el riesgo de daños por descargas electrostáticas.

■ Cualquier periférico o equipo utilizado con la Raspberry Pi debe cumplir con las normas aplicables en el país de uso y debe estar marcado en consecuencia para garantizar que se cumplen los requisitos de seguridad y rendimiento.

Para obtener todos los certificados de conformidad y sus números de registro, visite www.raspberrypi.org/compliance.

Svenska

Raspberry Pi 4 Modell B 1GB, 2GB + 4GB
VIKTIGT: BEHÅLL DENNA INFORMATION FÖR FRAMTIDA REFERENS.
Varningar

■ Alla externa strömförsörjningar som används med Raspberry Pi måste uppfylla alla tillämpliga regler och standarder i det land där de används. Strömförsörjningen måste tillhandahålla 5 VDC och ha en lägsta märkström på 3 A.

Instruktioner för säker användning

■ Produkten bör inte överklockas.

■ Utsätt inte produkten för vatten eller fukt, och placera den inte på en ledande yta medan den är i drift.

■ Utsätt inte produkten för värme från någon värmekälla. Den är utformad för tillförlitlig drift vid normal rumstemperatur.

■ Använd produkten i en väl ventilerad miljö, och täck inte över den vid användning.

■ Placera produkten på en stabil, isolerad yta vid användning, och låt den inte komma i kontakt med ledande föremål.

■ Var försiktig när du hanterar produkten för att undvika mekaniska eller elektriska skador på kretskortet och kontakterna.

■ Undvik att hantera produkten med strömmen på. Håll den endast i kanterna för att undvika elektrostatiska urladdningar.

■ Eventuell kringutrustning och utrustning som används med Raspberry Pi måste uppfylla relevanta standarder i det land där den används, och den bör märkas så att säkerhets- och prestandakraven uppfylls.

Besök www.raspberrypi.org/compliance, för alla certifikat och nummer om överensstämmelse.

EU Radio Equipment Directive (2014/53/EU) Declaration of Conformity (DoC)

We, Raspberry Pi (Trading) Limited, Maurice Wilkes Building, Cowley Road, Cambridge, CB4 0DS, United Kingdom, Declare under our sole responsibility that the product: Raspberry Pi 4 Model B 1GB, 2GB + 4GB variants to which this declaration relates is in conformity with the essential requirements and other relevant requirements of the Radio Equipment Directive (2014/53/EU).

The product is in conformity with the following standards and/or other normative documents: SAFETY (art 3.1.a): **IEC 60950-1: 2005 (2nd Edition) and EN 62311: 2008** EMC (art 3.1.b): **EN 301 489-1/ EN 301 489-17 Ver. 3.1.1 (assessed in conjunction with ITE standards EN 55032 and EN 55024 as Class B equipment)** SPECTRUM

(art 3. 2): **EN 300 328 Ver 2.1.1, EN 301 893 V2.1.0**

In accordance with Article 10.8 of the Radio Equipment Directive: The device 'Raspberry Pi 4 Model B 1GB, 2GB + 4GB variants ' operates in compliance with harmonised standard EN 300 328 v2.1.1 and transceives within the frequency band 2,400 MHz to 2,483.5 MHz and, as per Clause 4.3.2.2 for wideband modulation type equipment, operates at a maximum e.i.r.p. of 20dBm. The device 'Raspberry Pi 4 Model B 1GB, 2GB + 4GB variants' also operates in compliance with harmonised standard EN 301 893 V2.1.1 and transceives within the frequency bands 5150-5250MHz, 5250-5350MHz, and 5470-5725MHz and, as per Clause 4.2.3.2 for wideband modulation type equipment, operates at a maximum e.i.r.p. of 23dBm (5150-5350MHz) and 30dBm (5450-5725MHz).

In accordance with Article 10.10 of the Radio Equipment Directive, and as per below list of country codes, the operating bands 5150-5350MHz are strictly for indoor usage only.

BE	BG		CZ	DK
DE	DD		IE	EL
ES	FR	HR	IT	CY
LV	LT	LU	HU	MT
NL	AT	PL	PT	RO
SI	SK	FI	SE	UK

The Raspberry Pi complies with the relevant provisions of the RoHS Directive for the European Union.

WEEE Directive Statement for the European Union

This marking indicates that

this product should not be disposed with other household wastes throughout the EU. To prevent possible harm to the environment or human health from uncontrolled waste disposal, recycle it responsibly to promote the sustainable reuse of material resources. To return your used device, please use the return and collection systems or contact the retailer where the product was purchased. They can take this product for environmental safe recycling. Note: A full online copy of this Declaration can be found at www.raspberrypi.org/compliance/

⚠️ **WARNING: Cancer and Reproductive Harm - www.P65Warnings.ca.gov.**

FCC
Raspberry Pi 4 Model B 1GB, 2GB + 4GB variants FCC ID: 2ABCB-RPI4B
This device complies with Part 15 of FCC Rules, Operation is Subject to following two conditions:
(1) This device may not cause harmful interference, and
(2) This device must accept any interference received including interference that cause undesired operation.

Caution: Any changes or modifications to the equipment not expressly approved by the party responsible for compliance could void user s authority to operate the equipment.

This equipment has been tested and found to comply within the limits for a Class B digital device, pursuant to part 15 of the FCC Rules. These limits are designed to provide reasonable protection against harmful interference in a residential installation. This equipment generates, uses, and can radiate radio frequency energy

and, if not installed and used in accordance with the instructions, may cause harmful interference to radio communications. However, there is no guarantee that interference will not occur in a particular installation. If this equipment does cause harmful interference to radio or television reception, which can be determined by turning the equipment off and on, the user is encouraged to try to correct the interference by one or more of the following measures:
■ Re-orient or relocate the receiving antenna
■ Increase the separation between the equipment and receiver
■ Connect the equipment into an outlet on a different circuit from that to which the receiver is connected Consult the dealer or an experienced radio/TV technician for help.

For products available on the USA/Canada market, only channels 1 to 11 are available for 2.4GHz WLAN

This device and its antenna(s) must not be co-located or operation in conjunction with any other antenna or transmitter except in accordance with FCC's multi-transmitter procedures.

This device operates in the 5.15~5.25GHz frequency range and is restricted to in indoor use only.

IMPORTANT NOTE: FCC Radiation Exposure Statement; Co-location of this module with other transmitter that operate simultaneously are required to be evaluated using the FCC multi-transmitter procedures. This device complies with FCC RF radiation exposure limits set forth for an uncontrolled environment. The device contains an integral antenna hence, the device must be installed to so that

a separation distance of at least 20cm from all persons.

ISED
Raspberry Pi 4 Model B IC: 20953-RPI4B
This device complies with Industry Canada license-exempt RSS standard(s). Operation is subject to the following two conditions: (1) this device may not cause interference, and (2) this device must accept any interference, including interference that may cause undesired operation of the device.
Le présent appareil est conforme aux CNR d'Industrie Canada applicables aux appareils radio exempts de licence. L'exploitation est autorisée aux deux conditions suivantes :(1) l'appareil ne doit pas produire de brouillage, et (2) l'utilisateur de l'appareil doit accepter tout brouillage radioélectrique subi, même si le brouillage est susceptible d'en compromettre le fonctionnement.

For products available on the USA/Canada market, only channels 1 to 11 are available for 2.4GHz WLAN Selection of other channels is not possible.
Pour les produits disponibles sur le marché USA / Canada, seuls les canaux 1 à 11 sont disponibles pour le réseau local sans fil 2,4 GHz. La sélection d'autres canaux n'est pas possible.

This device and its antenna(s) must not be co-located with any other transmitters except in accordance with IC multi-transmitter product procedures.
Cet appareil et son antenne (s) ne doit pas être co-localisés ou fonctionnement en association avec une autre antenne ou transmetteur.

The device for operation in the band 5150–5250 MHz is only for indoor use to reduce the potential for harmful interference to co-channel mobile satellite systems. les dispositifs fonctionnant dans la bande 5150-5250 MHz sont réservés uniquement pour une utilisation à l'intérieur afin de réduire les risques de brouillage préjudiciable aux systèmes de satellites mobiles utilisant les mêmes canaux.

IMPORTANT NOTE:
IC Radiation Exposure Statement: This equipment complies with IC RSS-102 radiation exposure limits set forth for an uncontrolled environment. This equipment should be installed and operated with minimum separation distance of 20cm between the device and all persons.
Cet équipement est conforme aux limites d'exposition au rayonnement IC RSS-102 définies pour un environnement non contrôlé. Cet équipement doit être installé et utilisé avec une distance de séparation minimale de 20 cm entre l'appareil et toutes les personnes.

INTEGRATION INFORMATION FOR THE OEM

It is the responsibility of the OEM / Host product manufacturer to ensure continued compliance to FCC and ISED Canada certification requirements once the module is integrated in to the Host product. Please refer to FCC KDB 996369 D04 for additional information.

The module is subject to the following FCC rule parts: 15.207, 15.209, 15.247, 15.403 and 15.407

Host Product User Guide Text

FCC Compliance
This device complies with Part 15 of FCC Rules, Operation is Subject to following two conditions:
(1) This device may not cause harmful interference, and
(2) This device must accept any interference received including interference that cause undesired operation.

Caution: Any changes or modifications to the equipment not expressly approved by the party responsible for compliance could void user s authority to operate the equipment.

This equipment has been tested and found to comply within the limits for a Class B digital device, pursuant to part 15 of the FCC Rules. These limits are designed to provide reasonable protection against harmful interference in a residential installation. This equipment generates, uses, and can radiate radio frequency energy and, if not installed and used in accordance with the instructions, may cause harmful interference to radio communications. However, there is no guarantee that interference will not occur in a particular installation. If this equipment does cause harmful interference to radio or television reception, which can be determined by turning the equipment off and on, the user is encouraged to try to correct the interference by one or more of the following measures:
- Re-orient or relocate the receiving antenna
- Increase the separation between the equipment and receiver
- Connect the equipment into an outlet on a different circuit from that to which the receiver is connected Consult the dealer

or an experienced radio/TV technician for help.

For products available in the USA/ Canada market, only channels 1 to 11 are available for 2.4GHz WLAN

This device and its antenna(s) must not be co-located or operation in conjunction with any other antenna or transmitter except in accordance with FCC's multi-transmitter procedures.

This device operates in the 5.15~5.25GHz frequency range and is restricted to in indoor use only.

ISED Canada Compliance

This device complies with Industry Canada license-exempt RSS standard(s). Operation is subject to the following two conditions: (1) this device may not cause interference, and (2) this device must accept any interference, including interference that may cause undesired operation of the device.
Le présent appareil est conforme aux CNR d'Industrie Canada applicables aux appareils radio exempts de licence. L'exploitation est autorisée aux deux conditions suivantes :(1) l'appareil ne doit pas produire de brouillage, et
(2) l'utilisateur de l'appareil doit accepter tout brouillage radioélectrique subi, même si le brouillage est susceptible d'en compromettre le fonctionnement. For products available in the USA/ Canada market, only channels 1 to 11 are available for 2.4GHz WLAN Selection of other channels is not possible.
Pour les produits disponibles sur le marché USA / Canada, seuls les canaux 1 à 11 sont disponibles

pour le réseau local sans fil 2,4 GHz. La sélection d'autres canaux n'est pas possible.

This device and its antenna(s) must not be co-located with any other transmitters except in accordance with IC multi-transmitter product procedures.
Cet appareil et son antenne (s) ne doit pas être co-localisés ou fonctionnement en association avec une autre antenne ou transmetteur.

The device for operation in the band 5150–5250 MHz is only for indoor use to reduce the potential for harmful interference to co-channel mobile satellite systems. les dispositifs fonctionnant dans la bande 5150-5250 MHz sont réservés uniquement pour une utilisation à l'intérieur afin de réduire les risques de brouillage préjudiciable aux systèmes de satellites mobiles utilisant les mêmes canaux.

IMPORTANT NOTE:
IC Radiation Exposure Statement: This equipment complies with IC RSS-102 radiation exposure limits set forth for an uncontrolled environment. This equipment should be installed and operated with minimum separation distance of 20cm between the device and all persons.
Cet équipement est conforme aux limites d'exposition au rayonnement IC RSS-102 définies pour un environnement non contrôlé. Cet équipement doit être installé et utilisé avec une distance de séparation minimale de 20 cm entre l'appareil et toutes les personnes.

Host Product Labelling

The host product must be labelled with the following information:

"Contains TX FCC ID: 2ABCB-RPI4B"
"Contains IC: 20953-RPI4B"

"This device complies with Part 15 of FCC Rules, Operation is Subject to following two conditions:
(1) This device may not cause harmful interference, and
(2) This device must accept any interference received including interference that cause undesired operation."

Important Notice to OEMs:
The FCC Part 15 text must go on the Host product unless the product is too small to support a label with the text on it. It is not acceptable just to place the text in the user guide.

E-Labelling
It is possible for the Host product to use e-labelling providing the Host product supports the requirements of FCC KDB 784748 D02 e labelling and ISED Canada RSS-Gen, section 4.4.

E-labelling would be applicable for the FCC ID, ISED Canada certification number and the FCC Part 15 text.

Changes in Usage Conditions of this Module

This device has been approved as a Mobile device in accordance with FCC and ISED Canada requirement. This means that there must be a minimum separation distance of 20cm between the Module's antenna and any persons

A change in use that involves a separation distance ≤20cm (Portable usage) between the Module's antenna and any persons is a change in the RF exposure of the module and, hence, is subject

to a FCC Class 2 Permissive Change and a ISED Canada Class 4 Permissive Change policy in accordance with FCC KDB 996396 D01 and ISED Canada RSP-100.

As noted above, This device and its antenna(s) must not be co-located with any other transmitters except in accordance with IC multi-transmitter product procedures. If the device is co-located with multiple antennas, the module could be subject to a FCC Class 2 Permissive Change and a ISED Canada Class 4 Permissive Change policy in accordance with FCC KDB 996396 D01 and ISED Canada RSP-100.

In accordance with FCC KDB 996369 D03, section 2.9, test mode configuration information is available from the Module manufacturer for the Host (OEM) product manufacturer.

Australia and New Zealand
Class B Emissions Compliance Statement
Warning: This is a Class B product. In a domestic environment this product may cause radio interference in which case the user may be required to take adequate measures.